DECORATING YOUR HOME
WITH COLOR, TEXTURE, AND PASSION

Photographs by Brian Park and Paul Wright

Thomas Nelson
Since 1798

NASHVILLE   DALLAS   MEXICO CITY   RIO DE JANEIRO   BEIJING

Published in Nashville, Tennessee, by Thomas Nelson. Thomas Nelson is a trademark of Thomas Nelson, Inc.

Thomas Nelson, Inc. titles may be purchased in bulk for educational, business, fund-raising, or sales promotional use. For information, please e-mail SpecialMarkets@ThomasNelson.com.

Photographs by Brian Park and Paul Wright
Cowritten by Monica Haim
Chef: Mariana Velasquez
Graphic Design: Kiko Kairuz

Library of Congress Cataloging-in-Publication Data
Arcila-Duque, Juan Carlos, 1966-
  Latin style : decorating your home with color, texture, and passion / Juan Carlos Arcila-Duque ; photographs
by Brian Park and Paul Wright.
     p. cm.
  ISBN 978-1-4016-0365-6
  1. Interior decoration--Latin American influences. I. Park, Brian A. II. Wright, Paul. III. Title.
NK2115.5.E84A73 2008
747--dc22

2007038805

Printed in the United States of America
08 09 10 11 12 — 5 4 3 2 1

To my family, friends, and all the people who,
each in their own way, supported the idea of
bringing Latin Style to the American lifestyle

CONTENTS

Preface   vii
Introduction   viii

CABANA LIFESTYLE   1
Cabana Décor   7
Cabana Homes   11
Isla Rosa   13
Casa del Mar   23
Koralia Beach   31
A Caribbean Lunch   41

HACIENDA LIFESTYLE   51
Hacienda Décor   57
Hacienda Homes   61
Mountainside Hacienda   63
Tropical Hacienda   71
House of the Roses   81
A Gaucho Asado   91

PARADISO LIFESTYLE   103
Paradiso Décor   109
Paradiso Homes   113
Jungle Refuge   115
The Bamboo House   125
The Lily Pond House   133
Dinner in Paradise   141

PUEBLO LIFESTYLE   153
Pueblo Décor   159
Pueblo Homes   165
The Classic Pueblo House   167
The Colonial House   175
The Sanctuary House   183
Casa Mexicana   191
Roadside Celebration   199

Celebration Planning Tips   209
Acknowledgments and Credits   213

PREFACE

With this book I aim to deconstruct the generalization of the word "Latin" by giving it four distinct dimensions of visual possibility—each one infused by the magic and passion naturally encoded in the Latin lifestyle. After years of living in the United States, I learned to love the clarity and simplicity of the American manner. But a rediscovery of my Hispanic upbringing compelled me to enhance this modern lifestyle with a personalized Latin touch. I became part of a new generation of Latinos who are not only living the American dream but also *creating* a new, more dimensional, American experience—one built on the prospect of new culture, ethnicity, and flavor.

As a decorator and art collector, I find profound inspiration in all the people and places I experience. I trained in New York, worked in Europe, and employed this diverse palette of design experience in Miami. Through it all, I remained convinced that I wanted to shed my Latino past and evolve into my new and improved international self. But as I would ultimately discover: you can take the person out of Latin America, but you can never take Latin America out of that person.

I returned to my roots but with an appreciation and zeal for American practicality, that sturdy bastion of simplicity that has shaped countless generations of life and style in the United States. While I enjoy the nuances of what many consider to be an exotic style, I know how to employ that style within the framework of modern expediency—American practicality meets Latin flair.

This book is not about *one* place in Latin America—it is about *every* place in that exciting region. It aims to capture the spirit and dimension of the Latin aesthetic, the power of its details and traditions, and its unwavering, timeless chic. It is meant to serve as an evocation, an inspirational account to stir your senses and open your mind about style and design in your own life and home. I invite you to consider that practicality and fantasy can coexist beneath one roof.

INTRODUCTION

Each day here in America, the melting pot of ethnicity simmers on with new possibilities for culture. Technology allows us to experience every corner of the world in our own living room—we are global by virtue of our time. This social characteristic makes our choices more diverse and broadens our horizons when it comes to what is acceptable and viable in our homes. We travel to such places as Africa, India, or Thailand and return home yearning to again taste those flavors, to feel those sensations. So we wear more color, spice up our food, and adorn our rooms a certain way, consciously prodding our own sense of nostalgia and making what seemed like a fantasy an everyday reality. But even those whose travels are limited to the imagination can enjoy a bit of spice in their homes. With this book I explore a new approach to Latin Style, one stripped of cliché and defined by distinct visual and textural attributes that create very particular moods.

"Latin" has become part of the modern American experience, and the legacy of visionaries like Desi Arnaz, Oscar de la Renta, and Carolina Herrera has helped pave the way for a distinctly Latinized sense of success. Today, the creative momentum of the J.Lo generation continues, with such artists as Antonio Banderas, Ricky Martin, Shakira, and Selma Hayek swinging the gates of ethnic art and stardom further open.

In Latin America, everyday life is the result of familial social structures that have shaped over the centuries into intricate configurations of kin, a culture of grandparents, aunts, uncles, and cousins. The Latin way is characterized by reunions: food is made en masse, tables are set for feasts, and hosting is considered a veritable art. Because Latin America is a vast territory of diverse landscapes, it is a world that lends itself naturally to outdoor entertaining. A party is one thing, but a party on the beach or in a charming old house, in the jungle or on an estate—that is an entirely different sensory experience. Because of its inherent range, Latin Style can be both cozy and exotic. It lends itself to creative expression and a sense of optimism. Latin Style has the power to make every day a vivid celebration by helping us live more consciously and with a profound appreciation for the details. Regardless of our class or social stature, the Latin way means we cling to a natural zest for life. Through robust cuisine, colorful décor, and lively music, Latin Style helps us savor each moment of life with gusto no matter where—or who—we are.

Through my travels in Latin America, I became increasingly inspired by the vistas, colors, architecture, crafts, and people of the various regions, appreciating in each place the effortless way in which décor and lifestyle go hand in hand. I became rapt by this juicy world of color and smiles and nature and music. The nuances and quirks of each place sparkled for me, and the details of each one resonated as distinct but definitive characteristics of four specific moods. I wanted to somehow articulate the essence of this dynamic décor with more of an American sensibility, to create a design palette that was both exotic and approachable. I took it upon myself to organize and classify what has existed in Latin American style for centuries, and in doing so, these four separate ambient concepts emerged: *Cabana, Hacienda, Paradiso,* and *Pueblo.*

This mapping-out reconfigured my entire relationship to Latin Style; I could now apply American practicality to a more exotic visual context. For each concept, I decided to locate and decorate several homes that would each speak to a certain aspect of that overall theme. Through this process, I learned that each of these four lifestyles offers mesmerizing variety. As I explored the lines between fantasy and authenticity, the settings emerged as expressions of these nuanced décor motifs, revealing the heart of each place. In this way, each space for me became a slice of life, a story about a style.

In keeping with the age-old Latin standard of uninhibited joy, I decided that grand, lively celebrations would be the ideal way to conclude our exploration of each of the four concepts; after all, socializing and entertaining dictate the expression of Latin design. The goal was for the celebrations to express the soul of each concept, and these unique gatherings and special meals became yet another way to exalt the spirit of the spaces that we were creating.

As you will also see, when we categorize the design possibilities, color schemes begin to emerge, textures start to make sense for their given space, and the spirit and character of the true ambiance can authentically come to life. For example, the Amazon, a paradise of deep jungle, elicits a certain verdant lushness and mystery, while the Caribbean beaches create an aura of white calm and island life; similarly, the cobblestone streets and colorful old buildings of a pueblo reflect an urban folklore disparate from the old-world stateliness of a lone house on a faraway hacienda.

Of course, I do not expect my readers to convert their homes to Mexican villas; instead, I aim to offer and organize some of the brilliant nuances of Latin décor that I believe speak to some of the most spectacular attributes of a truly chic lifestyle. Once your senses understand what the four concepts entail, you can begin to personally customize your taste for all that is Latin and to select elements of each for your own specific scenario. It is my sincere hope that you will discover traits within each lifestyle concept that will speak directly to the moods you long to evoke.

To this end, my journey through Latin America became a personal scavenger hunt of inspiration, a living storyboard, so that I could distill the essence of each style concept and then translate it into a more practical sense of décor. Each place that I visited gave me visual information that somehow locked in with one or more of the four concepts I was beginning to explore. My inspiration came directly from collaborating with the local people, galleries, antique shops, and artisans to essentially celebrate the beauty of all their surroundings as I observed and participated in the aesthetics of their day-to-day life. As an interior designer, I was accustomed to outsourcing furniture and accessories for my clients, selecting exactly what I needed to make the space happen; for this project, I enjoyed the challenge of employing most of the elements that were already in the homes and communities to create flavorful stories about lifestyle and design in the context of American practicality.

My creative process for this book stems directly from my re-encounter with the vivacious splendor of Latin America: it begins with a profound appreciation for the panorama of the landscapes, gradually homes in to the regions and locales, and ultimately enters the rooms, nooks, and overall sentiment of the homes and people within. By internalizing the subtle gradations of tone that each place had to offer, detail for detail, I created a mental and inspirational blueprint through which to tell this visual story. The result of this personal and creative full circle is a book that fuses the social traditions of the Latin American cultural experience with a modern cosmopolitan lifestyle.

The process was made entirely possible by the cordiality of some of my excellent friends, and new ones made along the way, individuals who graciously opened their homes, kitchens, closets, and hearts, allowing my imagination free play. I had access to their linens, to their china, to all their accessories and finest objects. I worked with everyone in the household, including the housekeepers, and my own guest chef, Mariana Velasquez—collaborating with everyone to enhance the ambiance that was already there.

The goal of this book is to show how to use space, texture, and color to explore the basic visual philosophies that define Latin Style. The catch, of course, is that while many people might feel an affinity for all things Latin, when it comes to their own homes, they may not always know how to integrate these foreign elements without falling into preconceived clichés. However, by taking simple visual cues from this tradition, we can gradually evolve the culture of our own personal décor. The photographs and words that follow are the evocations that resulted from my own travels in Latin America and the limitless décor possibilities that I explored there. These images and their descriptions are meant to inspire the possibility and power of the Latin touch in any home. Consider them a way to gently but consciously move toward a Latin chic in your own life—one color, one texture, and one flavor at a time.

CABANA
LIFESTYLE

The sun is the ruler here in this world of pastels and seashells, where hammocks replace chairs and feet remain bare. The smell of fresh coconut traces the afternoon breeze, an air that is damp and salty, but always delicious on the skin. Time stands still in this dream of crystal seas and white sands, a permanent vacation governed simply by the culture of the beach and the rules of its natural warmth. Fresh seafood sizzles on grills as cocktails, frosty and tart, make the rounds. Massive hibiscus flowers open their petals like outstretched arms, and the distant jingle of a wind chime echoes in the breeze as the setting sun casts an electric pink into the fading blue sky. When you are in Cabana, there is simply nowhere else you would rather be.

HACIENDA
LIFESTYLE

The tradition of elegance is cultivated here, entire homes built on the prospect of leaving legacies by enjoying life. This is horse and cattle country—great lands of worn old leather and red wine. The homes are both rustic and refined, spaces designed on the basis of earthiness and elegance combined, where families have gathered for generations, surrounded by the natural beauty and the great horizon of mountains. The mist of the mountains blends with the smoke exhaling from the chimneys, while fireplaces begin to crackle as the evening stars make themselves seen. Black and white photographs hang like archives on the corridors of these grand estates, which stand like monuments of a family's mark in time.

PARADISO
LIFESTYLE

This is nature as naked as she gets: a lush raw jungle, fertile and green, at once abundant and stark. Organic minimalism reigns supreme, a décor of simplicity inspired entirely by the land and its resources. The gigantic trees cover and hover over the rain forest floor, where mysterious enclaves form naturally. The humidity trapped in these spaces instills each flower and plant with life, which seems to sprout forth from every crevice in the earth. The atmosphere is green and dewy, with a sense of stillness that is also somehow fierce. There is nothing here but earth and life, sound and sensation, night and day. Paradiso is a place for an adventure, an idyllic sanctuary in which to be lost.

PUEBLO
LIFESTYLE

Bold, bright colors punctuate an aura that is spicy, festive, seductive, and alive. The spirit is always up, the music is always on, the markets are always busy, and the people are always smiling. Folklore and tradition underscore all of life here, their details dictating the hues, flavors, and rhythms of each moment and each mood. Religious figurines, votive candles, and family portraits engender an almost sacred mood in the homes—poetically ironic against the playful and vivid tableau of revelry. In this vibrant landscape, no room or tabletop is ever too cluttered and every day bustles with family, friends, feasts, and fresh flowers.

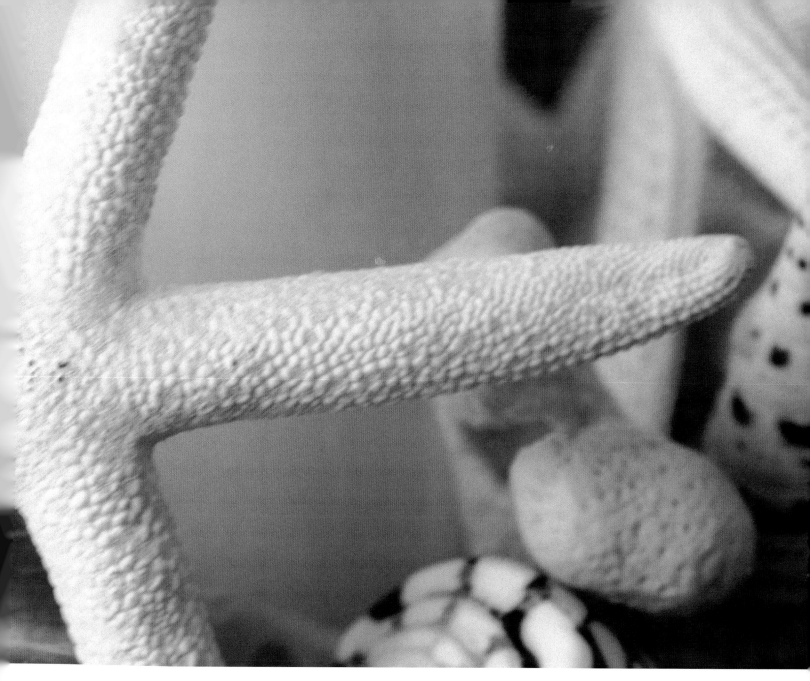

CABANA
LIFESTYLE

Summertime lingers forever in the Cabana lifestyle, where the omnipresent breeze conveys seaside tranquility. To live the Cabana lifestyle is to live the dream: a bungalow life lit by the vivid shades of aquamarine, where the crystalline sea dictates every creature's course of action and the sun casts shadows and light with romantic precision. Rhythm and beats give tempo to each day, the grooves acting as aural accessories to the infinite crashing of the waves on the shore. Cabana life is the reverie of al fresco showers, hammock naps in the afternoon shade, and the steady, hypnotic dance of a ceiling fan cooling the porch. Here, doors and windows remain permanently ajar and tattered piles of fishing nets lie entangled on docks and boats, a beautiful chaos of textures that tells the stories of the coast and its people. In this place, where neutrals converge chromatically with pastels in idyllic sun-washed afternoons, colors themselves signal the profound sense of relaxation that rules Cabana life.

In the Cabana world, sea salt flavors the air, as well as the tanned skin of the people who live here, and around every corner the sizzling crackle and aroma of foods deep-frying in hot oil awaken the senses. This is a place where the sunset is king, an everyday testament to the magnitude of the ever-changing skies. Here, the light moves across the expanse of white beach throughout the course of each day, accenting every morsel of the tropics with shadows and luminescence, creating an ambiance at once warm and coquettish. The squawking of seagulls punctuates the breeze, along with the intermittent lapping of water against boat bottoms in docks. The nectar of luscious tropical fruits brims in abundance, helping to fuel life in Cabana, a lifestyle that answers only to the elements—the sun, the sea, and the sand. Bare feet and frosty cocktails define the temperament of the day. Cabana is the place for a permanent vacation: the perpetual escape and the haven for total wellness.

A Cabana attitude can be found throughout Latin America, where destinations like the Dominican Republic, Cartagena, Cuba, and the Mayan beach paradise of Tulum express the quintessence of island life and Caribbean soul. Here prevails an exquisite fusion of European colonialism from the Netherlands with African rhythms, an aesthetic inspired by the possibility of paradise on earth and an indulgent expanse of white sand. A circumnavigation of the entire continent of South America shows a stunning sprinkling of beaches, each one shaped by the contours of its own piece of coast and, of course, the culture of the people who inhabit that country. Each locale has its own understanding and articulation of beach culture and coastal life, the distinctions between them fostered by their different topographies, inhabitants, and respective cultures. There are Playas Del Carmen on the Caribbean coast of Mexico; the Caribbean islands of Jamaica, Aruba, and Curaçao; Cuba and Puerto Rico; Punta del Este in Uruguay; Cartagena in Caribbean Colombia; and the coast of Brazil. Within this vast panorama of tropics and oceanside lie many gradations of beach and corresponding aesthetics. Actual coastal culture, for example, differs subtly from the lifestyle of more remote island regions. Despite their differences, in both iterations, the gallant palm trees stand asymmetrically as sentinels over the area, shielding the land and its cheerful residents and visitors from any sense of darkness or negativity.

Cabana offers architectural variations, beginning with the classic Jamaican experience, where colonial windows and expansive porches, a view of the ocean, and the swish of the waves become part of life both inside the house and out. In this calming meditative arena, rocking chairs sway on open verandas, facing the water in devout recognition of its import and majesty. High ceilings endow interior spaces with a light, airy atmosphere, blurring the lines between beach and home, creating a quiet euphoria, an unadulterated freedom. In its more tropical iterations, Cabana resides beneath a thatched roof and a gentle breeze, where the sounds of merengue, salsa, and reggae breathe rhythm into the late afternoons and nights.

CABANA
DECOR

In the same way that Hacienda and Pueblo are design concepts governed by the mountains, and Paradiso by the jungle, Cabana is indelibly linked to a life by the sea—be it on a small island in the distance or as part of the rugged coastline of a port town. In either case, the ocean dictates the rhythm of these locales, giving their inhabitants a distinct marine flair evident in their style of dress, the music they dance to, and their attitude toward entertaining and cuisine. An ease lingers here, a prolonged sense of tranquility, a feeling that the tide can actually wash away all of the day's trials and tribulations.

The quality of the light is amplified in Cabana, perhaps the result of a strong sun mirrored on crystalline waters, where high-contrast colors pop with saturation against white sands and baby blue skies. The waters themselves are nuanced: the Pacific Ocean flows more brusquely and intensely, with burly dollops of white foam asserting themselves on jagged rock formations, whereas the Atlantic moves languidly, calm and steady in her own pool-like blue-green. The sun, de facto king of Cabana, sets on the Pacific, sending new dimensions of chromatic possibility like streaks of paint into the sea, while an Atlantic sunset breeds a sky of neon pinks and violets—a lovely situation on either coast on any given afternoon.

Because the sun governs life in Cabana, the color palette includes washed-out hues, those muted, but somehow lively, pastels that seem to have faded into perfection with the comings and goings of the tide. Beige and aqua come together exquisitely in Cabana, inspired by a canvas of oceanic colors and the crispness of sky against water. This is a schema of blatant escapism, meant simply to warm the soul.

Cabana décor takes most of its cues from the sea, so its color palette also features

hues that mimic an assemblage of tropical fish, seashells, and coral. Together these colors come alive on land with an array of textures and sensations also derived from a life on the beach. Bright orange, yellow, and green sun-ripened tropical fruits make their way across entire beaches in massive wooden bowls carried by smiling locals dressed in crisp white clothes. Pinks abound, inspired by such natural objects as the innermost chambers of a conch shell, slices of fresh watermelon, and the messy tangles of fuchsia bougainvillea plants climbing on façade walls. Natural tones such as very light wood and very dark wood also serve to punctuate the exotic flora and marine environs, which explode in all shades of pinks, oranges, and violets—quintessential snippets of sunset bliss. These colors bring nature perpetually inside, creating an ongoing dialogue between the elements and the home.

In Cabana, the traditional notion of the plaza has evolved into the presence of a swimming pool in the courtyard, a private lagoon in the center of the home, surrounded by verandas and palm trees that seem to grow right through living rooms. Products of the sea are brought into the home, an evergreen interaction with one's surroundings expressed as design: a colossal shell on a credenza, a bowl of coconuts as a centerpiece on a table, tropical flowers strewn haphazardly on tabletops, outdoor showers made entirely of stones—all of these engender the dream of a beach-colored reality where less is always more. Hand-held fans made of natural fibers lie casually on tables and seating outdoors. Striped prints add marine character to interiors and exteriors alike, and found objects like starfish, seashells, and beach glass make their way into homes, where the coconut shell is used in dining utensils and décor accents. Sand dollars and pieces of coral interpose elements of the sea into the home, while rope elicits a maritime feeling, a romantic sense of what a life might be like if lived on a boat. Canvas, the fabric of sails, is also seen throughout. Sheer linen drapes billow in the wind, and breathable waffled cotton in whites and ivories complement the setting in any Cabana space. Houses are designed as comfortable respites from the tropical heat but, more important, as open-faced outposts from which to enjoy the breeze, the very breath and spirit of Cabana.

CABANA
HOMES

Given the various gradients of beach life that can exist, I tried to recreate three styles of Cabana and one celebration that, although each is unique, somehow collectively encompass the lifestyle's extreme nautical personality. The different approaches speak to the different types of colonization that occurred; the influences of Europe and Africa come together with the indigenous roots of these places, creating distinct visual lifestyles of the whole Cabana aesthetic.

The first home takes its inspiration directly from the island of Jamaica, that smoldering land mass in the Caribbean notorious for its saucy, sunny ways—an isle of candy colors, zesty flavors, wide smiles, and global rhythms, all stemming from a rich history of uprising, cultural resistance, and music.

The next setting is a more formal tropical beach house, taking its cues from islands like Cuba, Puerto Rico, or the Dominican Republic—places that show traces of Hacienda and Pueblo, given their colonial layouts of courtyards and plazas.

The third house lies on an otherwise abandoned beach, a desolate pristine expanse of sand and sea somewhere close to a rain forest, such as those in Costa Rica or Santa Marta.

The Cabana celebration is the quintessential oceanside affair, a tropical lunch set in what could be Punta del Este, Uruguay, or perhaps Cartagena, Colombia.

In these places, little towns near the sea and bay dignify a rich culture of fishing, where fresh seafood is a staple of the local cuisine. The advantage of being on an island is that you can have both a sunrise and a sunset, a detail never taken for granted, especially on those perfect afternoons of clear pool-blue sky and sea.

ISLA ROSA

The home stands like a personalized oceanic institution, a structure made for the lover of the sea, a place to entertain the notion that utopia is achievable through an everyday connection with the sky, sun, and sea.

This scene is inspired by the tropical beach life of island destinations like Jamaica, Antigua, or Curaçao, touched by the Dutch influence, but resoundingly alive with the pop colors of the Caribbean.

The setting calls to mind a feeling of youthful abandon at the water's edge, under a scorching sun that glows ceaselessly. Upon arrival here, you know with certainty that you never want to leave. The mass of ocean extends all around the house, where hammocks swing and planks creak under footsteps while the lapping of water beneath the deck below conjures the feeling of being on a boat. The home stands like some sort of personalized oceanic institution, a structure made for the lover of the sea. It seems to be suspended in that blue sea, alone on an expanse of wood. It is a place to forget about the rest of the world, to abandon reality, and to entertain the notion that utopia is achievable through an everyday connection with the sky, sun, and sea. Verandas on the upper levels of the home are carved intricately, in the tradition of the Dutch, each pattern transmuting different shapes of sunlight and shadow in and out of the house. A thatched roof covers the entire home, inviting the breeze inside, a true signature of the Cabana way. The thatch motif extends over the deck, creating graphic patterns of sunlight with shadows like pencil etchings all around the deck.

The roseate mood takes its cues from a row of lavender chairs in formation on a balcony and the fuchsia of the cocktail glasses—a cheerful hue reminiscent of flirting and vacations, a color that meets the blue of the sea in complete chromatic synchronicity.

Starchy white cushions and towels neatly folded on wooden loungers lie ready for

guests, who will undoubtedly sprawl there to enjoy ice-cold glasses of homemade lemonade and fresh sun-ripened fruits. Chairs and ottomans sit at the edge of the deck, just inches away from the liquid blue, near mats made of jute and straw, with candy-colored trim details, each one a personal oasis for horizontal lounging that puts a person eye to eye with the horizon. Sandals lie waiting near sturdy pink and white hammocks, where perfect naps leave one rested, sun kissed, and warmed on the inside.

The only sounds that matter are the lapping of the salty waves against the wood of the house, the creaking of those planks as bare feet move across them, and perhaps an old, scratchy salsa record playing somewhere inside the house. There is nowhere to be and nothing to do but bask in the good fortune of the moment by simply taking in its unrelenting beauty and calm. This is a place where the word "elegance" itself takes a break from the rigorous demands of its meaning, allowing instead a sense of casual chic to take over, leaving you endlessly refreshed and at ease, relaxed and revived.

CASA DEL MAR

This is a more grown-up island life in a place that caters to long, guiltless evening naps with the rumble of the sea snoring nearby.

This second style of Cabana evokes a more elegant island ambiance, a scene in a home somewhere in an old fortressed city, in a place that could be anywhere from Puerto Rico to Mexico, where Spanish-influenced towns near spectacular beaches are undeniably colored by that fortuitous proximity. The coastline is aggressive, the roar of the surf audible throughout the home, echoing within the old stone indoor courtyard, where from a lounging repose one can almost hear the repetition of waves crashing against the rock formations of the shoreline. This house is a magnificent structure of a home, with all of the spirit and inescapable leisure of the beach.

This is a more grown-up island life in a place that caters to long, guiltless evening naps with the rumble of the sea snoring nearby. Gone is the mess of sand and salt that comes with a day at the beach, and in its place lies an elegant tropical villa with a beach-side soul.

A great monolith of recycled white stone, the house beckons with indoor atriums, pools, and massive palms that make life indoors an outdoor experience. The design gives special attention to fresh open spaces, the home's white walls playing perfectly against the colorful furniture. Crisp reds and oranges pop against clean white walls and the blue of the pool, all the hues in harmony with the rustic character of the stone floors and the massive wicker baskets that are at once casually chic and endlessly functional. In a space such as this, there can never be enough greenery, and giant potted palms add seam-lessly to the indoor/outdoor tropical sensibility. This is the kind of place where tabletops can be personal altars—places to feature personal objects like found shells, coral, and candles alongside old books and fresh colorful flowers.

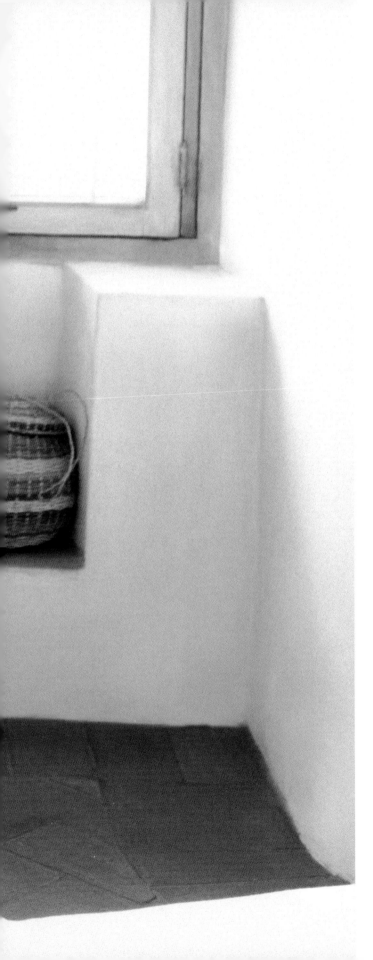

A grand table of dark wood graces the indoor/outdoor space, and the lush built-in banquette with its sumptuous cushions makes the area a perfect place for a tropical meal. Comfortable white chaise longues sit somewhere between the inside and outside of the house, where ceiling fans seek to temper the heat and humidity, a goal that can really only be achieved through a dip in one of the pools, where a Buddha statue might sit in meditative repose.

In this setting of ultimate leisure and rest, the afternoon hours take their time, each moment its own little slice of utopia, all of them comprising an idyllic tropical memory that lingers in the mind: a daydream on a terrace after a long day in the sun. On the horizon, the steeple of an ancient ruin encrusted in the fortress that surrounds the town stands out, the sun setting behind it all. Every day affords a new and spectacular view of the sea from this mystical fortress. And in this home in the middle of the old walled city, where the cold stone floors naturally soothe bare feet, there is the sense of a civilized encounter with the tropics, a feeling that these whitewashed spaces provide the ideal backdrop for high-end relaxation and rest.

KORALIA BEACH

Beyond this untouched vastness, the jungle pulsates, its smells and sounds alive in the air. By osmosis, it seems, the jungle resonates on the beach, the result a seaside experience that feels at once primitive and calm.

The final evocation for Cabana is a castaway fantasy, an idyllic slice of raw island life on a remote beach, practically abandoned—a pristine stretch of white powdered earth on which to rest and play, with only the striking blues of the sky and the sea for miles. These are the beaches that reflect the Spanish colonization, with the inhabitants' own interpretation of ocean culture emerging in structures such as the thatched roof huts that stand like open, tiny sea-pagodas along the beaches. Ruins of small boats abandoned dot the vast ivory shore, their old wood eroding in the sunlight each moment of each day. The scene is as rustic as it is tropical, and as sultry as it is calm.

Beyond this untouched enormity, the jungle pulsates, its myriad smells and sounds alive and circulating in the air. By osmosis, it seems, the jungle resonates on the beach, the result a seaside experience that feels at once primitive and calm. Jungle elements—coconuts and bamboo—comprise much of the décor here, a Cabana-Paradiso blend, if you will, that forges a raw encounter with the tropics. Though the landscape is sparse—ocean, sand, and sky—there is a sense that the passion of the rain forest is close enough to have an impact, its essence liable to spill from the canopies and onto the shores. This is a beach culture where bright colors meet simplicity, where any sense of décor is practically defined by its absence.

The setting is as much engineered for an adventure as it is for a good rest, an atmosphere that asks for all hands on deck, be it to manage the evening's bonfire ablaze on the shore or to assist with the abundance of green bananas to be hauled in from the jungle.

The tropical huts bear no walls, only a triangular thatched roof overhead, just a touch of a respite from the intensity of the sun. The huts' built-in seating areas cater to no-nonsense lounging in an ambiance of total escape, each one a tiny haven of bliss and stillness. Here, all the senses participate, taking in a welcome onslaught of stimulus and beauty. This is an entirely outdoor experience, a décor approach stripped of interiors in the conventional understanding. The look is clean, simple, and almost bare: instead of walls to divide rooms, curtains of colorful translucent beads clink and rattle with the breeze, the perfect aural complement to the ocean's roar. Straw hats litter the area, where orange cushions add punch to the space and no one objects to the mess of fishing nets draped about, or to the giant platters of limes, papaya, and fresh coconut, served in the morning and afternoon alike, the perfect tropical fare for a perfect tropical setting—all of it part of this Cabana castaway dream. This open, wallless space abandons any sense of privacy, forging a hiatus from daily life for a collective appreciation of honest seaside therapy.

A CARIBBEAN LUNCH

The space reflects a confluence of indigenous artistry, tropical flora, and marine life—a combination snapped into a life of its own with the added variables of percussive music and tangy cocktails.

I wanted the Cabana celebration to be entirely true to itself: a typical tropical Caribbean lunch, perhaps in a place such as the Dominican Republic or Punta del Este on the tip of Uruguay, regions classically notorious for their idyllic, postcard-perfect beaches. The beauty of life on the beach is that rich and poor alike have access to the natural bounty, so that celebrations come naturally for everyone every day. This celebration was consciously meant to be a no-frills approach to coastal culture. The way I understand it, by its very definition, the Cabana ideal demonstrates a chic simplicity, a built-in effect of the bountiful tropics. I envisioned a total sense of conscious informality, and more than anything, a genuine expression of coastal life through a stylish connection to its seemingly trite, yet fundamental elements. Coconuts, flowers, coral, fish, seashells: these very basics somehow together reveal a mosaic of the tropics that in the context of entertaining always brings forth a sense of joy and calm. Here, guests could arrive by boat for an ocean barbecue to coincide with the sun's final kiss before its descent for the night; they surely will not want to leave, what with the array of seaside delicacies and the visual panorama.

The table, dressed with runners of jute, is like an extension of the beach itself, accessorized with rows of seashells and coral tied to strings of raffia of various lengths. Heaping piles of sweet coconut rice and fried plantains make the rounds, both staples of the tropical menu of Latin America. Whole fried fish sizzles on the plates of guests, the quintessential entrée of the tropics. Pungent mojitos in frosted salt-rimmed glasses are passed around on large bamboo trays accessorized with seashells. The flavors fit perfectly with the tropical air.

A massive hibiscus flower sits perched behind someone's ear, glowing red, stunning alongside other equally fresh and crisp tones—the white inside of a perfectly ripe coconut, the clean green of a just-sliced lime. Lunch epitomizes the absolute freshness and bounty of a life on the beach; it celebrates the simplicity and beauty of that which comes most naturally to the region: fresh fruit, flowers, exquisite seafood, and the perfect climate. In this setting, any event—whether casual or formal—is rendered undeniably grand, as the elements stunningly lend an air of easy celebration.

The space reflects a confluence of indigenous artistry, tropical flora, and marine life—a combination snapped into a life of its own with the added variables of percussive music and tangy cocktails. Gone are the conventions of traditional table settings, replaced here with a laid-back, almost improvised, tabletop aesthetic, where plates are passed around casually and tropical trinkets keep the scene playful and fresh. This is the classic daytime affair, where guests inevitably return home feeling relaxed and refreshed, the scents of citrus and salt still faint in the air around them.

HACIENDA
LIFESTYLE

The elegant Hacienda lifestyle is not at all timid about its grandeur; it is a world originally shaped by the traditions of an old-world aristocracy, but elegantly revamped by the spirit of rugged earthiness—blue-blood splendor meets cowboy chic. In the Mexican Yucatan, the Argentinean pampas, Chile's rugged landscape, on the grasslands of Paraguay, and throughout Uruguay's pristine Punta del Este beaches, Hacienda's farm-inspired life gloriously thrives; and all through the Chilean wine region, areas like Zacatecas and Bajio in Mexico, and the coffee regions of Colombia there also lives a vibrant Hacienda aesthetic, a gaucho-like culture of ranches and barns and long, languid, lingering afternoons.

Grand old estates, or *estancias* can be found throughout Latin America, as physical testaments of entire family legacies. Their sophisticated interiors blend with the local mythology to create a sumptuous ambiance that feels at once lived-in and hospitable. Families and friends convene around fireplaces, in appreciation of the cozy elegance that the cold air can bring, forging their own sense of warmth through lounging and leisure.

The Hacienda ambiance expresses a romantic solemnity, where mountains, rivers, and wildflowers pepper a distant countryside and where silvery skies each day house a brilliant sunset, the parting gift of every afternoon. It is the perfect balance of luxury and leisure, of regal and rustic, where the presence of history gives shape to its atmosphere, warm and relaxed but simultaneously quite refined. The décor is oftentimes an homage to the Spanish heritage that left an elegant European impact throughout Latin America, evoking a vintage sensibility and a taste for the good life. However, the antiquated European character of the these homes is punctuated with indigenous Latin American touches, a testament to the place and the time of the homes' present reality and updated sensibility. In this way, the décor expressed in these spaces is also a visual testament to the convergence of cultures in the region and their aesthetic possibilities.

Equestrian chic permeates in Hacienda, its worn leather accoutrements scattered in harmonious disarray. Here, people are raised with the knowledge of how to properly mount horses, and stables are as much a part of the homes as are the fireplaces inside. Polo matches provide leisurely play, while acoustic guitars are strummed unhurriedly on patios.

On the vast, open grasslands, the façades of the estates wear climbing ivy like a beard on an aged man. High ceilings with exposed beams, ample balconies, sweeping stair-cases, and large open outdoor porches create dimension within the home, the epicenter of social gatherings. Spanish tile, stone walls, ornate windows, and hardwood floors stamp each home with age and character. Fine delicate dinner settings on long oak tables boast lavish spreads of tapas and pitchers of homemade sangria. The incandes-cence of heirloom chandeliers lights up a dining room with memories of the past, giving each home an air of tradition and nostalgia. Outdoor *asados*, social events where all varieties of succulent meats sizzle on smoky grills, lend themselves to hearty entertain-ing and give a whole new meaning to what we know as the traditional barbecue.

The Hacienda itself is almost like a character in the family, an aging relative that everyone adores and respects, to whom the rest of the family expresses its love by gath-ering at its feet in permanent celebration. The interior of this honored home harbors the entire family story, a visual archive of so many lives lived and shared: old books passed down from eldest to youngest; love letters on delicate paper hidden in drawers; some-one's found leaf dried and salvaged from the ground one perfect autumn day; the fam-ily's photographs, their art collections, their memories of so many summers and winters together. In this way, the Hacienda becomes a monument to their lives, immortalizing the spirit of an entire family legacy. Latin American culture is in many ways fueled by this emphasis on kinship, a passion that is translated into its décor and elaborate social life. This is especially true in Hacienda: from polo games and picnics to meandering horse-back expeditions and aimless forest walks, here the people converge to enjoy one another's company and to celebrate their sense of history as a family.

HACIENDA
DECOR

Hacienda means "estate" in Spanish, a definition that lends to the grand personality of what I like to consider a high-end ranch. Hacienda is Latin luxe and manages, with its vintage sensibility and unyielding love for the outdoors, to be cozy without compromising its aura of elegance. The graceful French and Spanish influence is at play in Hacienda, mingling with the rustic earthiness of indigenous Latin American cultures. Here, fine china and muddied cowboy boots combine well. The attitude can be festive and simultaneously meditative; it can be formal but somehow also stay fun.

The seeming inconsistencies of Hacienda are precisely the source of its charm: the notion of dark, worn leather, for instance, against the delicate smatterings of fresh-cut roses form a constant paradox of visual and textural styles that instead of clashing, somehow enhance one another—an infinitely balanced feminine and masculine presence throughout. Buttery leather, soft alpaca, luxurious cashmere—these are just some of the exquisite examples of the tactile experience that defines Hacienda; add to that the enticing aroma of steak slowly sizzling on an afternoon grill, while a sweet and frosty sangria is poured in rounds, and you have a world where the standards are high and the gorgeous, enduring afternoons are nothing but sacred.

Crystal chandeliers and tall dripping candles enhance a sense of deep romance inside the home, a lyrical, almost dramatic ambiance dignified by the many objects and memorabilia that decorate the interior. At the same time, cozy throws, pillows, and area rugs add warmth to spaces best described as idyllically snug. It is a home where the first rays of sun spill into a bedroom and awaken the sleeper, who then swings open the French windows and listens, in gratitude, to the arguments of birds or the distant gurgle of a stream.

The old-world Hacienda color palette of earthy browns plays with the confluence of past and present, inspiring turn-of-the-century nostalgia, a constant awareness of time and the mark it leaves. Throughout the wide-open grasslands and crop fields of Latin America, and through the rugged fields of the highlands, deep and earthy Hacienda colors emerge, colors that withstand the wear and tear of a rugged culture and a life outdoors. The palette evokes a dynamic cultural heritage and the presence of expansive and diverse natural landscapes.

The textures that comprise this lifestyle reflect the overall nostalgia and romance that give it meaning. Like fine wines and cheese, these textures refine with age; the worn tanned leather and dark rustic stained wood in a home tell the stories and hold the wisdom of many generations. These classic textures can be reinvented and reintroduced to spaces, endowing the room with a sense of history and clout.

Tanned leather of all varieties predominates in Hacienda, given the equestrian aspect of life with its ambiance of saddles and boots. These regions are also essentially cattle country terrain, where the consumption of beef is taken quite seriously, and animal skins then naturally become a part of many vignettes in the homes. Cow, goat, and deer horn also help create a rugged sense of elegance and beauty indoors.

Metals such as hammered silver, copper, and pewter are pivotal in Hacienda, as seen in almost every detail from the wrought-iron features of windows and doors to the many family photographs encased in silver frames that line mantelpieces and tabletops.

Hacienda is an experience of total convergence, where classic meets romantic, where indigenous craftsmanship encounters European élan, and where the softness of a brand-new rose plays perfectly against weathered leather. Jasmine flowers pepper the landscape, and other sensual materials like cashmere, alpaca, tweeds, and fine lace add dimensions of coziness, elevating the luxury levels in an otherwise earthy backdrop. Terra-cotta vessels and handcrafts reflect the region's wildlife and cater to an easy atmosphere of rest and relaxation. This time-honored quality of the texture scheme in Hacienda lends itself to a warm quality of glamour—one based on a taste for the good life, as well as a profound love of nature.

HACIENDA
HOMES

For this lifestyle to really emerge, I wanted to recreate a series of Hacienda settings that could just as easily be lost somewhere deep in the mountains as situated just on the outskirts of the city. The Hacienda lifestyle is weekend spirited, characterized by a feeling of remoteness and indulgent escape from the daily bustle of work and responsibility. When you are there, you are there to enjoy, period. This, to me, is the essence of Hacienda, and the scenarios that follow are in tribute to and inspired by that feeling.

The first home fundamentally tells the story of the classic cattle-ranch Hacienda, both rugged and refined, with its old colonial sensibility alongside pure equestrian chic. It is a place where the air is always slightly chilled and the nights are still and quiet, resulting in an atmosphere that is romantically austere.

The next home is essentially the tropical Hacienda, the mountain getaway with a sultrier side. This house could exist somewhere in Chile or in the coffee area of Colombia or perhaps outside Mexico City. It is close enough to the city that one would feel inclined to spend weekends there, but far enough away to ensure that those weekends become true escapes.

The third home depicts the more upscale Hacienda, characterized by a European attention to detail and a rich femininity in the form of enchanted gardens and lush, fertile vineyards. This is the Hacienda that thrives in the leisurely pleasantries of afternoon teas.

Finally, for the Hacienda celebration, I created a gaucho-inspired tableau, reminiscent of the pampas of Argentina, against a playful and energetic polo motif. Here, the spirit of young and old unite for a memorable afternoon of food, finery, and fun.

MOUNTAINSIDE HACIENDA

Courtyards with fanciful gardens are juxtaposed against the cowboy motif, and unruly tangles of plants crawl the estate walls, with the windows just barely peeking through the green.

The nearby mountains to this estate elicit the feeling of majesty, a jagged landscape where the colors of dusk and dawn manifest as a different kind of miracle every single day. A low-hanging layer of misty fog hangs around the mountainous panorama, like a giant smoke ring blown straight from the mouth of the great creator. This closeness to the mountains governs the life of this home, which, in turn, is governed by the sense of legacy etched in the home by the family. This process happens through an ever-revolving cycle of generational memorabilia, a culture of heirlooms, where objects passed down from parent to child become the building blocks of the décor palette. The items, though eclectic, complement one another, creating visual and textural dimension to each room of the Hacienda. The décor becomes less about the selection of the objects and more about their arrangement and display.

Life is self-sufficient in this Hacienda: produce grows right in the garden, cattle graze on the ranches, and sun-ripened fruit hangs heavy from the trees in the surrounding bush, ready to be served fresh for breakfast each morning. Here, one experiences a life fully and consciously connected to the earth. This Hacienda setting can be the distant enclave for an artist seeking inspiration or the home in which a family can reunite.

This cattle country estate, its walls rotting with time, could be tucked all along the Andean Mountains, stacks of smoke exhaling from its fireplace. Here, the chilly morning air carries the intermingled aromas of freshly cut flowers, roasting coffee, and leather saddles, while the afternoon breeze makes its way in with the scents of warm olive oil, grilled steak, and red wine. Every dawn is a majestic experience, and each dusk its perfect complement, the entire day a rare treat set against the distant mountains.

Lavish courtyards with fanciful gardens are juxtaposed against the cowboy motif of earth tones and rugged textures. Wrought-iron gates and entrances stand guard before grand studded wooden doors, and unruly tangles of plants crawl the estate walls, with the windows just barely peeking through the green. Massive doorways made of old, gnarled wood dramatize the spaces, enhancing an air of history and comfort.

Dark, earthy tones rule the interiors—from the handsome leather furniture to the exposed wood beams. The darker tones pop against the crisp white walls, providing an ambiance of virility to the spaces. The ample fireplace crackles alive as the de facto epicenter of the Hacienda, a place for family and guests to convene, to be warmed, and to take in the exquisite rugged beauty of this cattle-country oasis. This is the living room of ultimate coziness, where supple leather chairs and dark wooden floors create the framework for the ultimate lair of tranquility.

The dining area is a perfect example of the unique visual paradox that tends to characterize the Hacienda lifestyle: the delicate white linens on the table and the giant bouquet of lilies and roses in the center contrast with the dark wood of the dining table and the leather-bound chairs, an undoubtedly masculine setting with the very necessary feminine touches. The silverware with bamboo handles speaks directly to the Latin American character of the interior, soulful but not austere, the definition of the Hacienda lifestyle. Eclectic vintage clocks and urns passed down through the generations sit proudly on the mantel, completing the space. Treasured china is carefully arranged on the wall. These objects from the past add a sense of import to the area without compromising the space's natural warmth, which is the result of white walls perfectly balanced with chocolate brown wooden furniture. This dynamic creates an atmosphere that not only is interesting because it is textured, but also is comfortable precisely because of those textures.

TROPICAL HACIENDA

A masculine tone permeates every room, with an array of brown, terra-cotta, and earth tones, hunting accoutrements on proud display, and a general feeling of simplified décor in the living spaces.

The setting here somehow incorporates subtle traces of exoticism and simultaneous warmth—a Hacienda in the tropics, capable of so many different moods and possibilities at once. Surrounded by lush, verdant, well-manicured lawns, the house itself stands alone, a massive burnt orange edifice against a horizon of mountains, proud and elegant but also approachable in its look and demeanor. Gone are any aristocratic demands, replaced here by an earthier interpretation of "refined." The home is the hub of all social activities, naturally forging a sense of everyday communal life among its inhabitants and visiting guests alike, an outpost in the country where they may partake of life's very best. This home is built on the premises of tradition, the spirit of the outdoors, and old-world taste.

The unpretentious décor here is slightly conservative. Stone fountains and a mess of greenery wrap the house, with towering palms overhead, a stamp of the tropics standing tall in adulation of the sun. An outdoor sconce with a lion's face hangs over an ivory stone fountain against the imposing orange structure. The rooms within feel warm and sumptuous, offering a sense of being on vacation in one's very own space. Far from spartan, the feel of the home is easy but not overdone. The space actually feels as good as it looks.

A masculine tone permeates every room with an array of brown, terra-cotta, and earth tones, hunting accoutrements on proud display, and a general feeling of simplified décor in the living spaces. Elaborate wicker furniture plays nicely against the shimmering gold of a mirror frame; and religious paintings contrast unexpectedly with the masculine aura

that dominates most of the interiors. In the den, a chocolate-colored leather sofa, an old wooden chest, and a palette of browns all play against the femininity of the colossal crystal chandelier hanging overhead, posing coquettishly like the only woman in a room full of men.

Elaborate hand-carved wooden doorways offer an almost artisan feeling to the doorways of the spaces, each etching telling a different narrative, no two of them exactly alike. These grand entrances endow the rooms and the areas around these rooms with a distinct flavor of rustic chic. The floors are made of terra-cotta tiles or broad-planked wood, and the ceilings are high and generally exposed, all of these details coming together to create common areas that simply beg for an afternoon with a favorite book and a series of cat naps. In this domain, one naturally lounges, and giant, cozy wicker chairs with white cushions promise unremitting leisure and rest. It is a place elegant enough to inspire a sense of history, but casual enough in its demeanor and general spirit to invite warmth. Its earthy approach to color and texture plays beautifully against the overall pomp of the grand estate.

HOUSE OF THE ROSES

Here, one finds an atmosphere of total enchantment, a feeling that every inch of every garden and each detail of the home is engineered with an elevated standard of taste and class.

If Marie Antoinette had a Latin American alter ego, she would undoubtedly thrive here. In the same way that the previous Hacienda home carried an air of masculinity, this one does the complete opposite, with its soft feminized tone and highly European approach. This world of pinks, petals, and softness, toughened up with a bit of ranch culture, once again expresses the classic Hacienda duality—a perfect marriage of daintiness and grit. I staged this setting as the most genteel of all the Haciendas, an outpost of fine wines, teatimes, and formalized equestrianism. This is the Hacienda for ladies who lunch, an enclave of elegance where fresh flowers and perfect fare meet at every table indoors and out. Here, one finds an atmosphere of total enchantment, a feeling that every inch of every garden and each detail of the home is engineered with an elevated standard of taste and class, a true homage to the power and pomp of formality and tradition.

Historically and culturally, roses are ancient symbols of love and beauty, associated with Greek goddesses and even the Virgin Mary—testament to the fundamentally feminine character of this ever-sacred flower. In this Hacienda, the presence of fresh-cut roses en masse affirms this feeling of womanly grace and transforms an otherwise mannish estate into something unequivocally pretty. The gorgeous display of flora turns an old estate into a princess's dream. Even the contours of the house help elicit a more feminine aesthetic. Somehow soft, the building boasts fewer lines and more curves. The mingled smells of wine, wild roses, saddle leather, and delicious food circulate in the typical afternoon of life on this estate, a place known for its seemingly effortless and well-kept refinement.

A grand old corridor beckons with the assemblage of paintings and old lithographs that hang on its walls, a lively composition of memories and art. Flowers, long candles, and other objects of luxury accessorize the credenza, which is flanked by old, dark brown leather-bound chairs—again, that necessary hint of masculinity.

Inside, in addition to the dizzying bouquets in the vases, the detailed floral wallpaper and elaborate area rugs continue the images begun by the exquisite gardens outside, almost exaggerating the appreciation for flowers here. Their natural softness against the crackling embers in the fireplace creates a most idyllic afternoon setting for entertaining or repose. Antique chairs, also displaying the signature floral motif, this time in upholstery, work well alongside the buttery leather brown armchair, the whole vignette set with a gentle precision, the perfect scenario for an intimate afternoon tea. This is the fairy tale of unabashed elegance, a conscious display of luxury underscored by true finery and a precise focus on all that is grand. The setting is mature, a taste acquired over time.

A GAUCHO ASADO

It is the kind of day that lingers in the mind long after the day has ended, immortalized in the memories of the guests, who in its aftermath will reminisce longingly for those enchanted afternoon hours on that spectacular estate.

This celebration marries so many of the Hacienda themes, but the standout motif is the juxtaposition of young and old, illustrated by the upbeat vibrancy of guests enjoying a perfect day on an elegantly aging farm. This *asado,* a classic gaucho-inspired cookout, embraces tradition, but is laced with the modern sensibilities of the friends and family who unite for an afternoon of sports, companionship, and outdoor dining. The scene begins on a colonial estate, where open verandas and dramatic balconies overlook a garden of stone fountains and lush greenery, with the mountains on the horizon.

In this classic Sunday afternoon, nothing matters more than collective recreation, relaxation, and repast—the kind of day that lingers in the mind long after the day has ended, immortalized in the memories of the guests, who in its aftermath will reminisce longingly for those enchanted afternoon hours on that spectacular estate. One guest might remember the bristly texture of the black and white cowhide chairs arranged around the outdoor table; another might long for another taste of a succulent sausage grilled by the light of the first stars; a third might recall the smell of leather in the wood-paneled shed where the polo equipment was stored. All will undoubtedly remember the roasted aroma of a campfire and the sound of a bolero in the distance, those details that sealed for them an experience of unbridled sensory perfection.

The highlight of the afternoon is a polo match; a group of spectators lounge on a cowhide throw, lazily rooting for the players while enjoying a syrupy homemade dessert from an aluminum tin that someone's grandmother graciously sent along for the day's

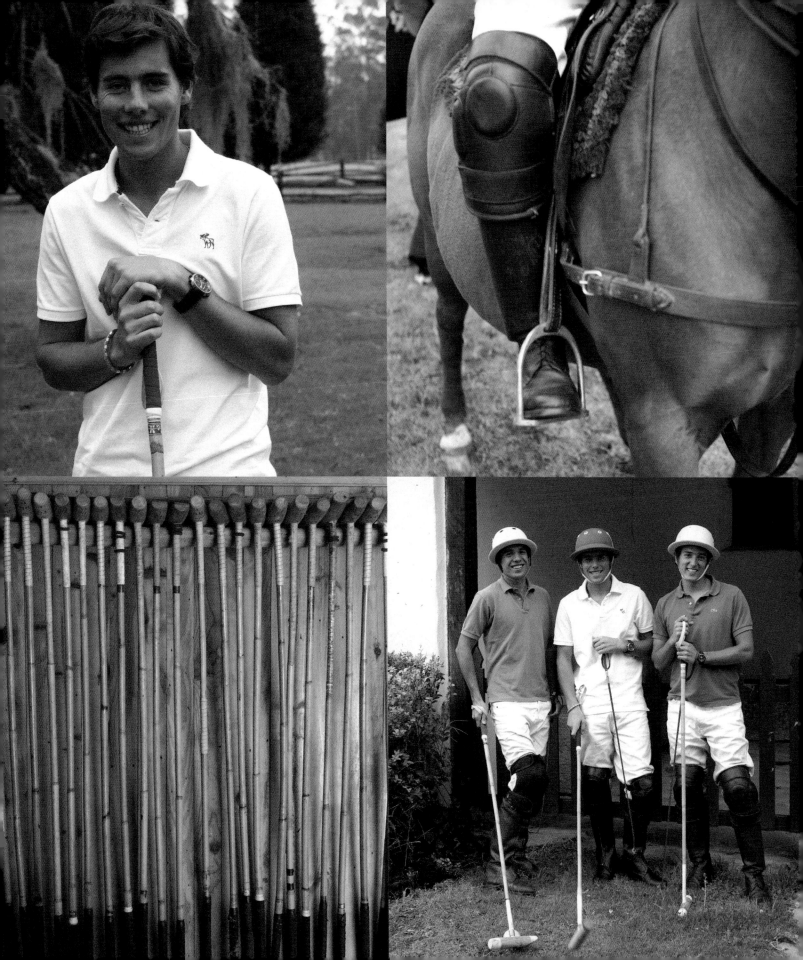

events. Woolen ponchos and riding boots lie strewn on the grass, and as the hours pass, the party evolves into a more intimate gathering, a new story being passed around with each glass of wine. Though the air is chilly, the vibe is warm.

While the match carries on in the background, a long table is set to perfection, and guests soon enjoy an ample feast of grilled meats cooked on an open fire and local wines whose grapes have matured on nearby land. Translucent burgundies illuminate glass carafes, green vines lie loose among the plate settings, and a vase filled with roses is the centerpiece of the table. Again, that fantastic and unexpected concurrence of roses and horses, a classic Hacienda blend, caters to both a male and a female sensibility. To this end, the celebration truly glorifies the dualities of Hacienda: young and old, athletic and refined, casual and upscale—all of them allowed to subsist at once in a scenario that is fundamentally governed by a regard for family history and the marvel of entertaining with class. These are the afternoons where bonds are formed alongside memories in a collective experience where everyone feels all their senses lit up at once.

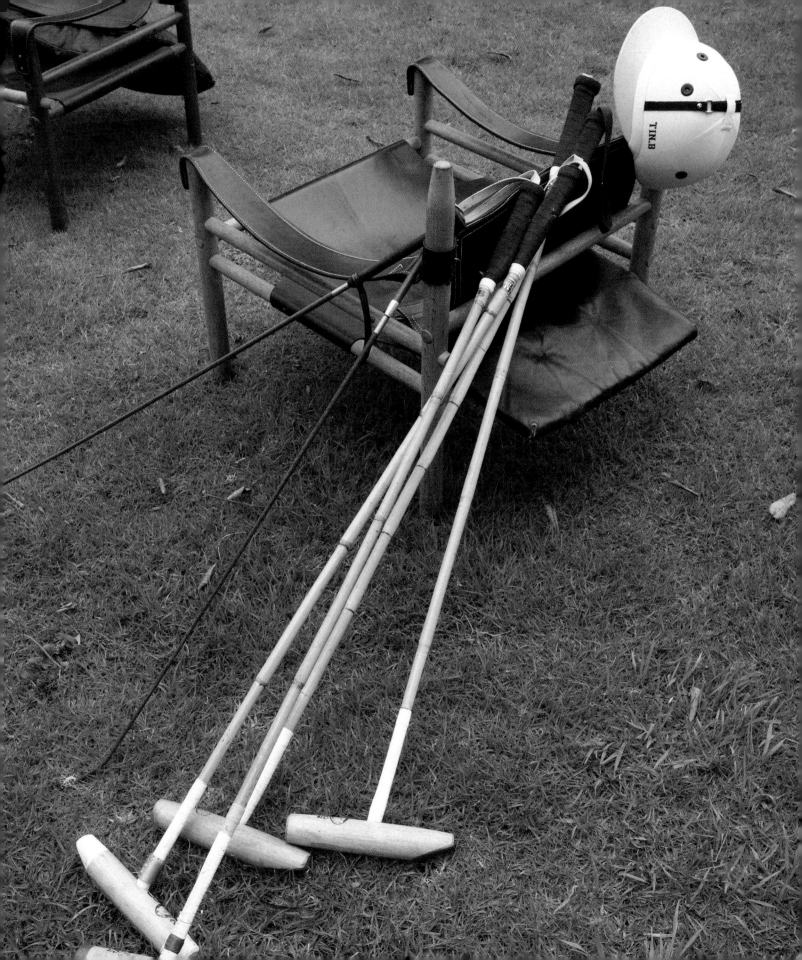

PARADISO
LIFESTYLE

Paradiso is the dream of unbridled exotica, a passionate fantasy of thatched roof verandas where the borders between the rain forest and the home dissolve into the misty air and colors appear as pigments in the autumnal light. From above, a sea of green appears, the leaves of giant trees protecting the tropical rain forest beneath. Massive rooftops made entirely of tree canopies encompass this secretive land, shrouding the area with mystery and creating a sweltering humidity that evokes a lust for adventure. Houses inevitably merge with the land, and the people—indigenous groups or primitive tribes—interact with and depend on this green treasure. Here lives the raw spirit of nature, a place where nuanced reflections are cast by the shadows and light of tree canopies, trickles of sunlight, and droplets of rain. The Paradiso lifestyle is the ultimate escape, the closest possible encounter with nature at its most primal, most fully expressed. Precisely this convergence with nature is what allows for such a raw, authentic expression of humanity. In this way, nature pretty much defines Paradiso décor.

The air is pregnant with the intoxicating musk of gargantuan flowers that look as though they could actually utter words, and the percussive intermittent sounds from wildlife create an aural matrix of echoes and silence. Birds traverse the treetops, their swiftly moving plumes appearing and disappearing as lightning bolts of color in the skies. Brooks gurgle in ravines below; their hypnotic, trance-like flow seems to feed the land with a sense of peace and calm. In Paradiso, there is an everyday sultriness, a sense that bare shoulders and feet are the way to nirvana.

Any land that has not been colonized by civilization in Latin America—from the Costa Rican jungle, the state of Chiapas in Mexico, and El Darien in Panama to Iguaçu in Argentina, Iquitos in the Peruvian rain forest, and Manaus in Brazil—is its own little slice of paradise, thanks to the climate. In this atmosphere people feel a profound connection with nature and its bounty. For Brazilians, for instance, life is about celebration, self-expression, and the appreciation for the natural mystique of the deep tropics; every moment is regarded as a sliver of perfection, and every day is a reason to rejoice. The jungle of the Amazon is sacred in this country, and major conservation efforts reflect the people's profound ecological consciousness with respect to this gem. The days are marked with gratitude for the natural abundance, and the nights with lively fetes that go on through the night.

Paradiso, a veritable Garden of Eden, celebrates a raw, minimalist palette of colors and textures that forge the experience of a deep sense of mystery. I would argue that Paradiso is the best-kept secret of the Latin American world, a sensuous enclave of extreme rawness. It is the ultimate escape from the mundane, an almost wild encounter with the earth and its elements. Here, everything is brilliant and bold, as impossibly beautiful orchids grow alongside the most rare of fruits, hanging en masse from the enormous labyrinthine trees. The dark, mystic lure of the jungle crystallizes the essence of green, and the elaborate flora create a dark, sexy space where the notion of wild can only be read as breathtaking. In this primitive mood, verdant life sprouts forth through every pore of the earth, while the distant sound of drums adds a natural cadence to each moment and every day. Nature and light give shape and meaning to life in Paradiso, where the region's roots and culture emerge directly from the earth's timeless splendor.

The undeniable influence of indigenous culture is paramount in Paradiso, an artisan's sense of life that, at its core, enhances the air of untouched beauty. Handcrafted objects in these places directly and consciously reflect the awe and appreciation the craftsmen feel for their surroundings; the people's understanding of beauty here springs from a deep sense of gratitude and respect for the bountiful resources and the natural world they have the privilege of inhabiting.

PARADISO
DECOR

I must confess that I have a soft spot for Paradiso. I love its drama alongside its simplicity. Almost every object for use or décor in Paradiso is made from a natural resource, be it a leaf, a stalk of bamboo, a coconut shell, a seed, or a flower. Paradiso is the notion of being cast away in the farthest reaches of the Amazon and forced to discover a décor palette that could arise only from using that which the jungle has to offer—survivor design at its most romantic.

Irresponsibly growing plants, a bramble of impetuous flora, flourish wherever they can find and suck in the light, and the Paradiso lifestyle demands that décor follow the lead of such lush, irreverent displays of green. Everything grows savagely, creating a thick mess of jungle that swallows houses whole into a wild matrix of exotica. The plants are mysterious and cheeky, like the heliconia who poses on her leaves, a seasoned supermodel in a fluorescent red gown. An entire patch of lofty bamboo stalks lean staunchly in one direction, almost like elders nodding in agreement, while a gang of birds-of-paradise shoots open, expressive hands in the surrounding green, each flower assertively pointing its fingers. A slightly ominous feeling also fills the air, the sense that a panther may be eying you from a distance.

In Paradiso, everything is pristine, and human hands have touched the earth for the sole purpose of survival, leaving the barest of imprints and creating a culture of sustainability that could have been passed down only through generations of preserved indigenous wisdom. Materials are recyclable, resources are abundant, and the spirit of conservation dominates as a direct reflection of the people's love and respect for the tropical jungle, one of the true living jewels of Latin America.

Around the exteriors of the homes, patches of interconnected trees seem to wrestle one another, vying for the attention of the sun, their shady canopy instilling the homes with green. As if that were not enough, outdoor porches stretch into the depths of the forest, actually blending the home with the earth, affirming its magnitude.

Inside the homes (though "inside" is relative here), objects are both functional and aesthetic. Pieces made by indigenous hands are designed and built for a purpose, but in their craftsmanship evoke the wonder of human creativity. All forms of wicker and other natural fibers contrast nicely with the endless green. Plantain leaves, palms, and orchids serve to accessorize in the home as well as in the wild, a testament to the natural abundance and multifaceted character of the environment. Other raw textures such as rope, beads, seeds, grains, and coconut shells accent spaces, helping create a primitive oasis with simple, organic touches. An elaborately carved gourd can be a serving dish, an instrument, or a piece of décor, and it is exactly this kind of resourcefulness that characterizes the entire Paradiso way. Simply put, Paradiso glorifies the power of creation. From the beauty of the biosphere to the elaborateness of an artisan's carving, creation is the guiding force of Paradiso.

This lifestyle gives way to a simple but bold color palette, paying direct homage to the elements of nature that shape it. Lush tropical jungles abundant with thick vegetation play home to the rainbow of fruits, flowers, and birds that create a living color palette of dramatic hues, which in the light of the rain forest seem to glow. In Paradiso, colors are understood first as pigments, robust and earthy hues procured by indigenous cultures from mineral or biological sources, such as the Mexican fruit *achiote,* which is used for red pigment.

Paradiso's texture palette communes directly with nature, organic patterns and sensations of touch emerging from details of jungles and tropical rain forests, all alive with the earthy nuances of each seed and its plant. Given the natural humidity and consequential climate of lush fertility, it is no wonder that most of the textures felt and seen in Paradiso come directly from the earth.

PARADISO
H O M E S

While my interpretation of Paradiso pays homage to all of the tropical jungles of Latin America, my muse for the lifestyle was in large part the Brazilian Amazon, that bastion of sensuality where the jungle and the beach, and countless different cultures, meet eye to eye under a hot sun. It is no wonder the country is the largest and most populous on the continent, as Brazil is a place of extremes on so many fronts. Traversed by the equator, the country endures intense tropical and subtropical climates, where flowers grow to gargantuan proportions because the pregnant air bears the most fertile of dews.

A strong confluence of cultures resides here, too, as the roots of the indigenous Indians intermix with those of the Portuguese settlers and African slaves. All these inhabitants surely connected in some way or another with their rich natural surroundings. This, from the Paradiso point of view, is the key to décor and everyday life.

The first setting is the home of a proud conservationist, a remote jungle dwelling focused fundamentally on the land, where the ecological design of everyday life mimics nature.

The next setting is deep in the Amazon valley, where a sense of natural magic falls with the mist on everything that grows. The home is tucked right into a wildly growing patch of bamboo, and its décor, in turn, speaks directly to this spectacular positioning.

The third home highlights the power of a totally organic approach to décor. It is essentially about the pleasure and simplicity of entertaining outside, as well as the art of truly integrating indoor living spaces with nature.

Finally, the Paradiso celebration becomes a kind of civilized safari in the middle of the jungle. With the sense that no one is around for miles, the fete is based entirely on its innate remoteness and mystique.

JUNGLE REFUGE

To understand design in this context, there must be a willingness to abandon it altogether, forging a raw connection to nature, a conscious green minimalism for the home.

In many ways, this Paradiso setting is defined by its organic starkness: the elements of nature are the very building blocks of the design scheme. The itinerant trees known as the "walking palm" surround the home; their roots actually move on the earth, causing the whole tree to wander the jungle for eternity. The light in this place also shapes the look and feel of the décor, which essentially mirrors that which is naturally there: earth, plant, sun, and shadows. To understand design in this context, there must be a willingness to abandon it altogether, forging a raw connection to nature, a conscious green minimalism for the home. The décor here elicits the feeling that nothing is around for miles, a sense of desolate chic, of natural expanse and nothing more.

The home serves perfectly to depict the resourcefulness that emerges from the Paradiso approach, one that does not try to be chic—it just *is* by virtue of its simplicity. Here thrives the powerful idea of permaculture, an ecological design philosophy based on the premise of sustainability, which essentially means that man can survive perfectly with the natural abundance of nature's schema: mangos hang heavy on the trees for us to harvest, and the pit of that fruit is given back to the earth to continue the cycle, a permanent culture of flow with the land. The fruit is served almost primitively on broad, dark green leaves—no need for plates, no need for forks, just a raw encounter with nature's work.

Passion fruits lined up lengthwise in rustic wooden bowls offer tabletop visuals, but are meant also to be enjoyed—another display of the form *and* function model that characterizes the Paradiso lifestyle. Coconut shells become candle votives, and colorful

area rugs woven in jute provide a sense of home to the spartan jungle setting.

The elements are tribal, perhaps as homage to the African influence of the slave populations brought to the country. The décor palette, a vivid array of earthy, natural tones, reflects the people's desire to stay connected to their roots by taking their inspiration directly from their own ancestry and their ever-diverse heritage. When the sun sets, drums reverberate through the night, as embers from a communal bonfire spit and vanish into the starry dark. Here you imagine that an ancient African ritual may have occurred; it is a place for a mystical encounter through a dance with paradise.

To create such a setting, I distilled the essence of ecological design, organic elements, and nighttime mystique, turning to natural resources and the palette of nature as the ultimate source of inspiration and guidance. Objects such as trees, with all their details—the leaves, the wood, the canopy shadows and shade—become the building blocks for a space stripped of any frills. The resulting ambiance is a mysterious but natural calm, based on the premise of stark jungle chic.

THE BAMBOO HOUSE

The sun sparkles through bamboo configurations; as the tropical wind moves, the light each time hits different spots on the jungle floor, creating shimmers of gold in a kaleidoscope of green.

Here, bamboo becomes a mystical bridge, a labyrinth of green that transports a person from one magical spot to the next. Imagine a house nestled in the rain forest, sitting on a hill, its façade facing a giant patch of bamboo stalks that shade the deck. A simple trellis is suspended over the porch, wrapped in vines, as if the forest means to lovingly ensnare the whole house. Stone steps embedded in the earth form a pathway that leads into the heart of the jungle, where towering banana leafs and guadua stalks compete for real estate. Considered the most important variety of American bamboo, guadua is widely employed for construction by both the rich and the poor of Latin America due to its durability and sustainability. With low water requirements, guadua burgeons in full force, forming walls of green throughout the jungle.

The sun sparkles through these bamboo configurations; as the tropical wind moves, the light each time hits different spots on the jungle floor, creating shimmers of gold in a kaleidoscope of green. Giant papayas dangle from trees above, their sweet milk oozing from within as they ripen toward perfection. Soon they will be sliced open to reveal an orangey rose—the color of breakfast here. But for now, guest chef Maria Velasquez arranges tropical fruits in a wooden bowl. Knowing that the Paradiso table is defined by all things organic, she utilizes the fruit selection here as the very basis of the dining area's visual scheme. These fruits are the staples not only of tropical diets but also of the décor.

Deeper into the forest, tiny configurations of green dot a nearby pool of a pond, an amphibian world thriving within. The place resembles an ancient bath, where gods and

goddesses might have converged for a soak. The black water's reflective surface seems a sheet of glossy black tile in the midst of the jungle's vast carpet of green, a giant mirror in a mythical garden. In this organic neighborhood, capuchin monkeys trapeze through the canopies, howling their maniacal laughter into the night, while massive dragonflies trail spirals of purple, perhaps charting their course through the thick tropical air.

The nearby home is filled with crafts made solely from nature's bounty, natural fibers woven by hand into any number of household objects or pieces of art. Short, heavy logs of upright wood are used as side tables next to the chunky wicker furniture, creating the illusion of tree trunks growing right in the common areas. Every item in the house seems somehow to be of the earth, an overall unprocessed character that feels totally humble and pure. This setting is like a veritable time warp, infused with a sense of the prehistoric that is infinitely expressed in its artful simplicity. The space thrives on its essential spirit, which is a fundamental union with the earth around it.

THE LILY POND HOUSE

In this magical clearing in the middle of the jungle bush, the trees disengage their embrace and the open tributaries of the great Amazon River harbor entire worlds of biodiversity, a whole other realm of life and beauty, where caimans and alligators slither in the black depths.

To articulate ideas about Paradiso décor presents a challenge, as the lifestyle is practically defined by its absence. This house evokes the fantasy of an isolated jungle enclave, the farthest reaches of the jungle where you might imagine ancient mystics converging for metaphysical debates. The story of Paradiso is like *Alice in Wonderland*—except that this Wonderland is hidden somewhere in the tropical Amazon, brimming with giant water lilies that open and close at will. In this magical clearing in the middle of the jungle bush, the trees disengage their embrace and the open tributaries of the great Amazon River harbor entire worlds of biodiversity, a whole other realm of life and beauty, where caimans and alligators slither with catfish and piranhas in the black depths. This is a scene that could perhaps emerge from someone's dream of the jungle, an abyss of absolute mystery, silence, and stillness, where water lilies reign like queens over an expanse of wet gardens, blooming and closing, and confounding anyone who beholds the numinous process. This is a place to escape to, surrounded only by the myriad calls of the wild and air so highly oxygenated one cannot help but take profound, nourishing breaths though the day.

Ancient Egyptians and Indians observed that the lotus flower responds to the presence or absence of light and warmth, submerging itself by night and rising from the water at dawn, a sun salutation. Perhaps this is the underlying motive of the Brazilian species of water lily known as *Victoria amazonica*, whose leaves reach six feet across and can support the weight of a full-grown adult. A chemical reaction heats the inside

of the flower to a temperature exceeding that of the surrounding air, helping to disperse the bloom's sweet perfume.

In this setting, color is limited, reduced to a simple mélange of white façades, terracotta Spanish tiles on the roof, and other warm, earthy tones throughout the spaces, both indoor and outdoor. The green of the jungle is the color star here, enveloping the home in a luscious and consistent tone. The surface of the water, in turn, reflects this verdant resplendence, as well as the crisp blue sky under which the whole setting glows.

From the open deck of the white-walled house, on the chaise longue facing the water, one can behold the splendor of the water lilies on their impressive green pads, each one waiting for just the right moment to come into its full expression. Not unlike the first Paradiso house, the décor here is defined by its absence, allowing such phenomena as the water lilies, the bright blue sky, the stillness of the water's surface, and the colors of the sunset to stand out as the main elements of design. The feeling of the place is deeply meditative, with the expanse of river stretching into what seems like oblivion from the perspective of the deck chairs

DINNER IN PARADISE

The meal has an almost tribal air, a feeling of ceremony. Next to the dark ceramic plates, instruments made of seeds and shells lie still, suggesting the prospect of music or dancing at the meal's end.

For this gathering I envisioned some semblance of a civilized safari, where guests could sample a touch of the primitive in a setting of unadulterated natural chic. This would be a party in the middle of nowhere, with nothing and no one around for miles.

A pleated green leaf, massive and symmetrical, fans across the expanse of the table, where a tribal buffet of the freshest provisions is served on all varieties of fibers and woods. Piquant *ceviche* made with fresh tilapia appears in small piles on sea grape leaves, while votive candles burn in wicker holders, the light gleaming through fiber patterns, an incandescent glow for an otherwise dark ambiance. Scents of freshly fried plantains and grilled shrimp blend with biting citric aromas of lemons and limes, while the kick of the peppers awakens a whole other dimension of the olfactory experience. Here, one sees every part of the palm tree incorporated into the setting and the meal: its wood forms the structure of the house, its leaves are used as serving plates, the heart of the palm is sliced and served in a fresh salad, and finally the milk of the coconut that sprouts from the palm is used to stew the vegetables and fish.

The meal has an almost tribal air, a feeling of ceremony. Next to the dark ceramic plates, instruments made of seeds and shells lie still, suggesting the prospect of music or dancing at the meal's end. Citronella torches burn on the periphery, lighting and protecting the guests from the uncertainties of night beyond the trees, the whole table enveloped in the light of fire and the mingling smells of food and drink. The light of the moon through the trees forms shadows and light across the table, casting the evening with mystery. The air is heavy, but the mood is light, the guests delighted at the prospect of a celebration in such far reaches of exotica.

PUEBLO
LIFESTYLE

Color finds its purest, most dramatic expression in the towns, or pueblos, of Latin America, where the urban bustle converges with folklore and magic, and everything is illuminated by the art of exaggerated adornment. There are pueblos everywhere in Latin America—from San Miguel de Allende in Mexico to Lima and Cuzco in Peru, San Cristobal in Venezuela, Antigua in Guatemala, and the old city of Cartagena in Colombia. These places emanate a larger-than-life air of pageantry, a welcome sensory overload. The spiritual trinkets, crafts, baubles, and fabrics reflect the people's daily devotion to even the tiniest details of their beliefs—the organized clutter carries myth and lore, as the past and the present walk hand in hand.

The presence of God underscores every moment of every day; the people express their faith in this principle through their devout Christianity and through their love of life, both of which are reflected, down to the tiniest details, in their homes. That love is also articulated in their robust cuisine, music, and arts, and in the sense of perpetual celebration. Every moment is marked by jubilation—but with a certain air of tranquility.

Old houses with interior courtyards line irregular cobblestone streets, each balcony replete with a unique personality, flowers dripping forth with bursts of uncut color and spring-like urgency. Ancient churches with gold altars are lavishly decorated. Rustic architecture weathers the strong sun, which in turn, casts an afternoon slumber in the form of siestas. In Pueblo, even the details have details, as tireless craftsmanship reigns supreme.

Legendary artist Frida Kahlo, the great muse supporter of the Pueblo aesthetic, was famous for fusing realism, symbolism, and surrealism in her work. She brought a sense of whimsy and play to the style that very much gives shape and color to the Pueblo look today. Another influential artist was the muralist Diego Rivera, Kahlo's husband, who was also a serious endorser of big, bold, unabashed color. His work, like that of Kahlo's, was loaded with narrative and inspired much of the energy and passion evident in the Pueblo perspective. In this atmosphere, every object has a story to tell and every day is exalted; people exist in a heightened state that seems possible only against such a fanciful backdrop.

The same energy also moved the legendary Mexican architect Luis Barragan, one of the most notable architects of the twentieth century, to pioneer a style that combined modernism with colonialism and pre-Hispanic architecture. Barragan was profoundly influenced by the European sense of minimalism, which he saw as a perfect match for his own Latin American inclination to incorporate nature and authentic colors into design. The traditional layout of the Pueblo, as crafted by the Spanish, always included certain elemental characteristics, a common urban layout that prevailed from town to town. Always at its center was the church, the heart of the Pueblo, the axis on which life revolved, and its surrounding plaza, the soul of the town, where afternoon strolls provided serenity. The Pueblo was always located in the vicinity of a river and was usually also surrounded by mountains, enhancing the air of sanctity and natural abundance.

Pueblo décor is an intricate fusion of mestizo, Spanish colonial, and African influences, a stylistic mélange that emerged through the new racial iterations and flavors that arose after generations of different kinds of people intermingling. It is a style that consciously stays connected to the past through a glorification of the present. Simple wooden furniture is dressed up with flowers of all varieties in playful patterns; rooms are stocked with colorful, glazed pottery; and kitchens brim with old wooden utensils worn from generations of use. Pressed glass and colorful embroidered cotton textiles are used generously, and polychrome wood keeps it all young at heart. Accessories show strong pre-Hispanic Indian influences, creating meaningful vignettes that reflect history, while the candles and lace instill a sense of intimacy rooted in the present. Everything is consciously over-accessorized, generating a sense of abundance and joy. No color scheme is too outrageous and no tabletop too ornate, here in this world of elegant whimsy.

PUEBLO
DECOR

The overall look and feel of Pueblo can be infinitely vivacious and self-assured. The house exteriors combine a bold use of color against stacked stone, creating neighborhoods built on the basic premise of playful ornamentation. The entrance to every house boasts a unique individuality; one has a sense that if the door could talk, it would narrate a detailed account of the secrets that belong to the family behind its walls. Wooden blinds open and close through the day, allowing life inside the house to flirt casually with the activity of the cobblestone streets below. Courtyards, fountains, and plants lend to the general enchantment, and the proximity to the mountains also fosters a sense of the divine.

Inside the Pueblo home, the feeling is one of bountiful whimsy, an atmosphere of frenetic harmony, where it is somehow okay, and perhaps even encouraged, for objects and colors to clash—in fact, they come to life best when they do so, against a rich textile culture of natural fibers and hand-embroidered masterpieces. The consistent repetition of stripes and patterns throughout these elaborate pieces evokes the rhythmic nature of life itself, each stripe and each stitch a gesture of the artists, a sliver of their realities.

Color, in essence, defines Pueblo style. It emerges in slabs of intense saturation. Every vignette reveals some kind of rainbow, every color its own strand of personality in the genetic makeup of that house. Lively, unabashed green tones instantly bring to mind a busy street market and artisan culture in constant celebration of life. Colors reflect all the shades of bougainvillea, ranging from bright purple and hot pink to sunny yellow and flaming orange. The palette is also inspired by the fusion of desert and tropical climates. Vivid turquoise blues and spicy reds on tiles, pottery, and walls play against the earthy neutrality of terra-cotta floors, urns, and tableware. Fresh-cut flowers, magnificent little candies, and confections of all varieties create a sense of everyday abundance. The beauty of the Pueblo color palette is that colors don't necessarily have to work with one another to work with one another. The point is more to play with the edges of brightness and boldness, forging a mood of fun and festivity. The impact of the Pueblo color scheme is conscious—it naturally wants to be that vivid, as it takes its cues directly from the celebratory lives of the people and the stunning landscapes that surround them.

Tiny amulets, votive candles, and religious sculptures dress most of the Pueblo surfaces, micro-objects charged with a sense of sanctity and tradition. In this atmosphere, the details gradually spawn a character that becomes the nature of that space. One senses that no space in the home is taken for granted—every little nook and cranny is visually accounted for.

A rich and earthy tactile experience exists in Pueblo décor, as textiles and embroidered fabrics essentially drive the home interiors, while materials such as stone, exposed wooden beams, painted wood, and rustic brick provide the foundations. Adobe brick, too, is a classic Pueblo building block and one of the most ancient materials ever used for construction. This natural material, shaped and then dried in the sun, originates from sand, clay, straw, and other fibrous materials.

In Pueblo, flowers and plants are also key textures, bringing every window to life and life to every window, and adding an organic burst of color everywhere they bloom. Extreme color is always a magnificent thing to behold—but when it comes in the form of a beautiful cluster of flowers, it can instantly light up any space. Rooms are detailed with white linen and woven blankets, and embroidered pillows lie strewn about. In the bedrooms, cotton sheets are embellished with ribbon or woven accents. Flat-weave cotton rugs and different-sized baskets add a cozy warmth to the living spaces, and multicolored hammocks hang casually in the gardens.

Perhaps the presence of religion and church in the Pueblo scheme engenders a feeling of celebratory gratitude, a profound appreciation for life that finds expression in lavishly set tables, energetic colors, and indigenous craftsmanship.

PUEBLO
HOMES

The variances within Pueblo, as within all the other lifestyle concepts, reflect the layout and climate of each region: crisp mountain air feels markedly different from the sweltering humidity of the tropics, and so forth. The power of sunlight, or its absence, also helps shape the cultural DNA of a place, so that each area ultimately has a built-in barometer for what the aesthetic of day-to-day life should be like inside, and outside, the home.

The first Pueblo home, with its prototypical Andean atmosphere, is the perfect place for a family to gather and enjoy the long-established tradition of sharing fresh hot chocolate beside a cozy fireplace. This house could be in Bogotá, Colombia, or Lima, Peru, or any Pueblo characterized by its proximity to the mountains and the cold air that comes with them. This is classic Pueblo, although slightly more upscale than the more festive styles we will explore elsewhere.

The second home calls to mind a Pueblo in the tropics, places such as Cartagena in Colombia, and San Miguel de Allende in Mexico, where the balmy breezes from the beach sneak their way into the homes, mingling casually with the folklore celebrated within.

The next setting is also in the mountains, but the air here is warmer, allowing for perennial perfect temperatures. This farmlike Pueblo scene could be somewhere in Guatemala, Costa Rica, or perhaps El Salvador.

The fourth Pueblo home is in a more arid climate, still in the mountains, but influenced deeply by the folklore of Mexico and its street art.

For the final celebration, my goal was to create a party in a typical *tienda*, or "little shop." I wanted to evoke the sense that we simply stopped off the road somewhere and found a Mexican *tienda* in which to host a party that would pay homage to the magic and charm of Pueblo.

THE CLASSIC PUEBLO HOUSE

This is a culture of gatherings and fireplaces, where stories and remembrances are exchanged over the sensual elixirs of red wine and hot chocolate.

It is dusk, the gloaming hours, on what could very well be a Saturday. A chill is in the air, the sky a milky cerulean, and leaves on the trees shiver, anticipating the night ahead. The courtyard, usually active with footsteps and their echoes, now lies quiet and still, with only the rustle of plants slightly shifting. People begin to settle inside their homes, preparing for the evening's events. The mood first seems melancholy and nostalgic, until the cheerful flurry of sights, sounds, and smells strikes us as we open that grand old door.

Once over the threshold, we leave the world outside that home in the distance, and within those walls a haven of familiar comfort instantly emerges. The terra-cotta tiles throughout the house help foster a sense of play in the otherwise austere mountain atmosphere, and the indiscriminate arrangements of fresh-cut flowers add the soft sense of a garden indoors. Here you leave your worries at the door and take in nourishment from the good company and delicious food.

This is a culture of gatherings and fireplaces, where stories and remembrances are exchanged over the sensual elixirs of red wine and hot chocolate. To the ancient Mayan Indians, the cacao plant was sacred, giving life to what they considered to be the drink of the gods, so it is no wonder that so many generations later, throughout Latin America, fresh hot chocolate continues to thrive as a hallowed point of convergence for family gatherings. In this way, convening to drink chocolate is a modernized ritual of ancient wisdom and lore.

A gastronomical altar, the table offers tiny dishes and plates that serve to glorify the coming together of relatives. This sensory onslaught of all varieties of sweets and savories, such as delectable pastries confected by hand, samplings of cheeses, pastes of guava, and perfectly wrapped tamales, is a purposeful feast of tastings and treats, the Latin American equivalent of the British high tea.

In this high-end Pueblo, a pedigree of aesthetic dignity is handed down from parent to child. The delicate, hand-painted china appears and reappears on a multitude of tables over the years, passing through the different hands of many generations and worthy of countless family anecdotes and lessons. Through these meals and gatherings, the family's history is shaped and reshaped, its customs and traditions kept alive in a continuous loop of shared experiences. Religious paintings on the walls affirm the respectful, nostalgic undercurrents of the home, reminding those gathered there of their roots, and the lyrical sentiments are enhanced by the sound of a guitar strummed on the balcony, a perfect moment for anyone there to partake of it.

THE COLONIAL HOUSE

A casual, but festive, ambiance can contrast beautifully with the aging stones that comprise the buildings, ivy climbing their walls like green tentacles searching for the sun in their ascent.

This setting blends the notion of beach into the concept of Pueblo, bringing to life a colonial aesthetic surrounded by, and perhaps swallowed by, the tropics and all that they bring. Though the mountains are inevitably nearby, so too may be the beach, endowing to the space a warmer quality of air, loosening the energy within the home, and freshening the décor that emerges from these topographic variances. In this region, a casual, but festive, ambiance can contrast beautifully with the aging stones that comprise the buildings, ivy climbing their walls like green tentacles searching for the sun in their ascent. Burnt oranges and all shades of yellow color the walls, set golden against the large terra-cotta tiles of the floors.

This is a place where inner atriums and courtyards are replete with turquoise blue pools and overflowing fountains, every corner accessorized with smatterings of verdant tropical lushness, the whole scene evocative of an ancient ceremonial bath. The pool is as much a part of the interior décor as are any of the actual furnishings, homage to the sultriness of the tropics, despite the prevailing Pueblo sensibility. Sunlight aggressively streaks its way into the houses and courtyards through open windows and archways. Here, there is a concept of the "old city," a colonized township surrounded by an old fortress, its ancient stones wrapping the place with a sense of protection. Within these forted walls, festivities ebb only in the morning hours, when the sunrise majestically appears in its chaos of neon pinks and oranges from behind one of those magnificent archaic walls.

Doors and windows swing open and stay open, the warm air making itself at home, as much a part of the space's energy as its décor. Tall, engraved candelabras flank an

antique crimson banquette, a regal splash of Europe in an otherwise tropical setting. Tall candles melt as the hours pass, casting warm pools of light in unsuspecting places and sculpting small wax testaments to the passage of time and the power of mood.

The façade of the old colonial Mexican-style house looks almost like a ruin or an enchanted castle, with its gigantic archways and ancient stone columns. Hammocks hang in spaces that lie somewhere between the interior and the exterior of the house, the boundaries made blurry by the presence of flora and green and the pervasiveness of the humid tropical air. This same air colors the paint on the ever-fading walls, encasing the home with a sense of time and history. Nothing is polished about these interiors; worn and natural, they could almost be exteriors. The feeling inside the house would be somewhat cavernous where it not for the elegant mélange of accessories, such as the white embroidered hammock that hangs regally in the dark, exotic common area. This touch brightens the space and further defines its laid-back essence.

THE SANCTUARY HOUSE

This is the Pueblo where candy colors show up together on fanciful textiles embroidered with love, and where rich, extravagant fabrics offer brash concoctions of color and imagination.

This Pueblo home basks in the warm mountain air, as found in cities like Antigua in Guatemala or Lima in Peru, where the majestic jade peaks in the distance seem capable of enchanting the people in their midst. This is a *finca*, or farm-style Pueblo, with colorful rocking chairs swaying in cadence on open verandas, where the epic panorama of the mountain range can be properly taken in. Here is the Pueblo house of ultimate devotion to nature and to the universe, a sanctified space of healing through simplicity and warmth. This is the Pueblo where candy colors show up together on fanciful textiles embroidered with love, and where rich, extravagant fabrics offer brash concoctions of color and imagination. Their playful geometric patterns have an almost psychedelic quality, popping with intensity, like brand-new crayons on crisp white paper. Here, that white is cotton and linen, against which these electric hues are especially charged. The white in this context lends itself to an overdone spiritual tableau, providing a backdrop of calm and stillness for a vivid chromatic display. These are spaces where one can sit and reflect, homey environs that foster not only comfort and long meditative afternoons, but also social gatherings. This is the kind of Pueblo where one wants to be lost—a place to hone one's mindfulness, an oasis of tranquility.

An impassioned sense of Christianity is evident in this emotive space that is at once calm and quirky, brushed with a sense of fun, but always respectful in its visual execution. The rooms within are treated like little altars, with small amulets, crosses, hearts, and photos throughout, visual blessings and prayers, tangible affirmations. Diminutive bottles of tinctures and oils line up in wooden cabinets, in keeping with the general sense of

enchantment and ritual that tends to take over. Candles burn in careful multilevel rows, praise for the Virgin, whose mournful gaze is cast throughout the interiors.

The white built-in adobe spaces meet superbly with chunky furniture, reflecting a sense of lounging and leisure, while the massive cactus plants in giant terra-cotta urns infuse a desert quality to an otherwise mountainous vibe. Raw, exposed beams keep the feeling handsome and rustic, while the colorful hand-embroidery of the textiles ultimately brings out Pueblo's more feminine attributes. In the bedroom, an array of lit candelabras ignites a feeling of spiritualized coziness, bathing the grand suite in an almost divine, incandescent glow. Here, a small living room within the bedroom lends to the "clutter of chic" that defines the space. In the foyer, a shrinelike tableau of small objects gives light and personality to the space. The amulets, photos, and crafts sparkle in an impressionistic array on the wall. Beneath them on the console, a large wooden bowl sits as the centerpiece, cradling a gnarled bramble of fresh fruit. The arrangement is a perfect example of Pueblo's sense of passion and lore.

CASA MEXICANA

Each little piece of minutiae represents some aspect of the inhabitants' passion—be it spiritual, familial, celebratory, or simply an expression of personal aesthetic sensibility.

This final setting in the Pueblo style is pure majesty, a tropical refuge with towering green mountains on its horizon. The influence is Mexican, with the consistent use of burnt orange, yellows, and terra-cotta enhancing the brightly hued fabrics that also abound. These textiles, with their bold chromatic patterns and stripes, speak directly to the standard of artistry and zest for life that is part of the heritage of the region and a testament to the natural whimsy of everyday life. Each little piece of minutiae represents some aspect of the inhabitants' passion—be it spiritual, familial, celebratory, or simply an expression of personal aesthetic sensibility.

While the quintessential Pueblo townsperson may be perceived as humble, there is nothing shy here about the use of color; here the imagination is encouraged to explore, so the fantastical quality of the chromatic scheme directly mirrors the sense of play that shapes the Pueblo attitude—joyful, proud of its culture, and clearly not afraid to express itself. From the fresh produce and flowers brought in from the countryside to the hand-woven goods and artisan crafts, Pueblo takes its stylistic cues directly from the spirit of bliss that fuels its everyday life.

This house in the mountains is not oppressed by humidity and instead lies in a drier climate, reminiscent of the nearby desert. Its wide doorway of gnarled wood features a massive old lock and elaborate iron knockers that show the face of an angel-demon. The roof is thatched, a touch of the exotic for otherwise humble interiors. Inside, the décor is casual, an earthy expression of color and natural texture. Here, the spaces are created in a direct relationship with the landscape and its views. Entire living scenarios

are designed with the nearby mountain vista in mind. The common area finds its heart as a massive open-air pagoda, with tropical wooden furniture and hammocks dressed in white cotton, swinging in relaxed formation. During the day the sun peeks through the thatch in tiny shards of light, and in the evening, votive candles cast a glow on creative folk art, such as a collection of delicate, hand-painted pottery. Colorful, hand-woven pillows line the white canvas sofa, each one with its own distinctive pattern and personality. The coffee table, too, wears a runner in that classic, vivid pattern of Mexico, a certain Baja sensibility chromatically expressed on wool. Dramatic plants like palms, birds-of-paradise, ginger flowers, and palm trees are excellent in spaces such as this, where desert and tropics somehow overlap.

Eclectic objects like birdcages add to the natural but lively ambiance, which simultaneously promotes endless tranquility and enjoyment. At this tropical desert house, the mood is cheeky and upbeat, the music is loud, and the biting scents of cilantro and citrus hang thick in the air.

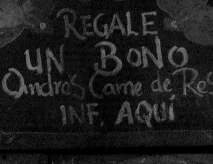

REGALE
UN BONO
Andrés Carne de Res
INF. AQUI

ROADSIDE CELEBRATION

I wanted this to be a place that would invite the possibility of anything, where the boundaries between food, art, and décor could be obscured by the sense that food can be both art and décor.

My vision for the Pueblo celebration was to create some kind of fantastical fete at a typical roadside *tienda*, the Latin American rendition of the "general store." But I wanted my gathering to somehow also be charmed with a feeling of exotic jubilation—an experience designed to activate every one of the senses all at once. I envisioned an overflowing Mexican cantina as if cast with a spell, with metal dishes shaped like fish and all varieties of crafts and trinkets hanging from ceilings like marionettes. I wanted this to be a place that would invite the possibility of anything, where the boundaries between food, art, and décor could be obscured by the sense that food can be both art *and* décor. In accordance with this vision, the artwork amplifies the textures of the succulent tastings that seem to emerge effortlessly from some sort of magical, ever-cranking kitchen. From this kitchen emanate the sounds of simmering and steaming stews intermingling with the clinks of pottery dishes and old wooden spoons, the regular cacophony of a little culinary factory. This is a world where the kitchen is a focal point and all food is a tasty expression of love, each dish and each morsel an ode to the power of people gathering together and the possibility of gastronomical perfection every single day. The Pueblo kitchen is alive, an ongoing furnace of activity and a hotbed of delicious aromas swirling together to tantalize anyone who passes by.

The atmosphere is that of an enchanted junkyard transformed into an adult playground, a phantasmagorical display of raw indigenous artistry, such as elaborate wrought-iron candelabras and fences displayed so that the revelers cannot really tell where one ends and the other one begins.

Fallen confetti, tiny colorful testaments to the festivities, lies strewn across the vast,

oak tabletops, where small dishes are alive with the colors of fresh, wholesome food. Piquant salsas in robust shades of red and green are peppered through the spread, alongside plates of homemade tortillas, the manna of the Mexican diet. Small terra-cotta dishes stacked in meandering, irresponsible piles become part of the table's surface, a florid canvas of culinary bustle.

Massive calla lilies sit at the helm of the table, which is a giant sensory collage composed of indigenous crafts and endlessly shifting edible tableaus. Every plate seems to have another little side plate, creating a matrix of sauces and spices. The tall wooden shelves are lined with precise rows of translucent tumblers, an arsenal of glassware that will be useful for the party, but with its shimmering reflections, will also serve as a pretty backdrop for the night itself. The electric atmosphere is pure Pueblo, where the people's understanding of life as a celebration fuels their every moment. From the artwork to the cuisine, the magic is in the details of this kind of space, where eating, drinking, and celebrating fuse into one consistent experience of joy.

Celebration Planning Tips

Tips for a Caribbean lunch:

- Use nature to decorate—place coconuts and limes on plantain leaves, and arrange tropical flowers loosely on tables.

- Consider colorful translucent cocktail glasses, like blue or green, to amp up the festivities.

- Tie your favorite seashells and starfish to strings of raffia to use as decorative table runners.

- Adorn your serving platters with fresh citrus—thinly sliced oranges or lemon wedges.

- Spice up your beer by pouring it into a salt-rimmed glass and adding a few drops of Tabasco and a teaspoon of lime juice. The result is a delicious michelada.

- Don't forget the classic mojitos with Bacardi rum.

- Serve coconut rice, the ideal accompaniment to fried fish, and a staple of the Latin American coast.

- Prepare plantains. This versatile tropical fruit can be baked, steamed, fried, roasted, or grilled.

- When purchasing whole fish, always ask which variety came in fresh that day; look for clear eyes on the fish and flesh firm to the touch.

- Surprise your guests with *cocadas*, the sweet Caribbean solution to avoid wasting any part of the delicious coconut. *Cocadas* are made with sugar (dark or white), dried coconut, and sometimes other fruits such as guava, pineapple, or papaya. They are best served with potent black Colombian coffee, my favorite kind.

HACIENDA
LIFESTYLE

Tips for a gaucho *asado* (barbecue):

- As an aperitif wine, try Carmenere, a fabulous red grape variety grown in Chile.

- Be sure to use a vintage-looking lace tablecloth with antique china and silver vases for your fresh flowers.

- Look for "dry aged" beef, a personal favorite; aged beef develops a wonderful flavor and tender texture.

- Season the meat with coarse salt, such as kosher or sea salt.

- Never, ever overcook your meats.

- Once the meat is cooked to the desired temperature, allow it to rest for at least ten minutes; this allows for the juices to stay in the meat rather than escaping when you slice.

- Grill some chorizo; no *asado* is complete without this zesty sausage.

- Think simple for salad: fresh tomatoes, lettuce, and onions dressed with vinegar and olive oil.

- Offer your guests *arepas*, the corn cake stuffed with fresh cheese or meat of which both Venezuela and Colombia both proudly boast and which they serve as bread at breakfast, lunch, and dinner.

- Serve a zesty sauce like a *chimichurri*, a blend of parsley, garlic, vinegar, and olive oil—the finishing touch of any complete *asado*.

- Research interesting Latin desserts like *cuajada,* a soft molten sweet cheese dessert melted with *panela*, or raw sugarcane.

- Enjoy the fireplace after dinner with my favorite scotch, Dewar's.

PARADISO
LIFESTYLE

Tips for a dinner in paradise:

- Dress the table with nature: large leaves, for example, make excellent runners.

- Surround the table with citronella torches to enhance the air of mystique and to keep the mosquitoes at bay.

- Tie sea grass around crispy white napkins to make textured holders.

- For a real organic touch, serve your courses on rustic wooden plates.

- Arrange fresh, colorful fruit in a large wooden bowl as a luscious centerpiece that is both edible and elegant.

- Use edible leaves to serve small dishes or finger food; consider serving sea salt in a small loose pile (as opposed to the traditional shaker) to enhance the raw, primitive ambiance.

- Remember the votive candles, which add to the air of mystery.

- Select freshwater fish such as tilapia, a mild and versatile crowd pleaser.

- Skewer fresh seafood like grilled shrimp for a perfect utensil-free dish.

- Serve *ceviche*, fish and shellfish marinated with lemon or lime juice. Garnish with crunchy vegetables and herbs.

- Offer plantain chips—*centavitos*—dipped in sour cream with peppers to soak up the juice of the *ceviche*.

- Delight your guests with passion fruit and Grey Goose vodka cocktails in tall glasses adorned with leaves and string, ideal with a menu of fresh seafood.

PUEBLO
LIFESTYLE

Tips for a Mexican celebration inspired by an enchanting roadside cantina:

- Make use of calla lilies, sunflowers, and jasmine flowers to enhance the table for a grand Pueblo meal.

- Assemble candles and religious figurines throughout the table for an air of celebration and spirituality.

- Become inspired by street food from such cosmopolitan cities as Mexico City or Tegucigalpa to create a dynamic party menu. Try *esquite*—a dish made of cooked corn kernels with mayonnaise, chili powder, lime juice, and cheese—or a jicama salad with radishes, turnips, and cucumbers sprinkled with chili powder.

- Avoid older chilies when shopping for dried chilies; make sure your merchant receives shipments frequently.

- Serve warm tortillas throughout the meal. Tortillas, the bread of Latin America, are the basis for wonderful interactive dishes like fajitas, whose assembly depends entirely on one's own personal taste.

- Offer refried beans and sour cream, perfect accompaniments for tacos, tostadas, and enchiladas.

- Roast tomatillos to make a sauce that can be served over shredded chicken accompanied with tortillas.

- Remember that not everyone has the same threshold for spice; offer a range of hot sauces, from mild to super hot, and serve them in small wooden dishes.

- Serve palomas, cocktails made of one part Corzo tequila from Bacardi and one part grapefruit juice, in sugar-rimmed champagne flutes for an enchanting touch.

- Explore different kinds of tequila mixers, such as sangrita, a blend made of orange, tomato, and chile juices.

- Surprise your guests with colorful confetti.

ACKNOWLEDGMENTS AND CREDITS

For supporting this project to bring Latin Style to the American lifestyle, I thank: my literary agents at Dupree Miller: Jan Miller and Nena Madonia and their staff; my publishers at Thomas Nelson: Pamela Clements, Brian Mitchell, Beth Hood, Damon Goude, Jennifer Greenstein, Geoffrey Stone, Gabe Wicks, Kristen Vasgaard, Casey Hooper, and all the staff; photographer Brian Park for his extraordinary work and patience; the team at Metal Monkey: agent Liz Padilla, talented photographer Paul Wright, his assistant James Hayworth, and stylist Luigi Carruba; agent Andrea Montejo for her support in finding a talented writer, Monica Haim, who was able to transcribe all my ideas; graphic designer Kiko Kairuz for his support and loyalty to the project; chef Mariana Velasquez for bringing flavor to some of the images of this first book; Lila Ochoa, Ana Maria Londono, and her assistant, Mariana Osorio, from Fucsia Magazine for their fashion support; Luis Velazco and Javier Delgado, the team behind the video camera; my licensing agents at the Cherokee Group: Sandi Stuart and Anthony Damiani; branding gurus Claude Salzberger and Ana Gonzalez for their creative advice and support; my editor at the Miami Herald Home and Décor magazine, Sarah Harrelson; Hispanic Magazine's Daniel Eilemberg and Adrian Saravia; Michael Honablue, Macdara Bohan, and Marlon Johnson at Plum TV; Leslie Ahrens, Jovanka Clares, Alejandro Reglero, and talented composer Descemer Bueno at EMI Music Publishing Latin America; Adam Nelson and his staff at Workhouse PR; Glenn Albin at Ocean Drive; Bacardi; Lexus; Alexis Summer for her support and for believing in me at the beginning; editors Jen Renzi and Dan Rubinstein; photographers Dora Franco, Mauricio Velez, and Claudia Uribe; Ben Moody for his ever-insightful advice; Angela Montoya at Colombia es Passion for opening her Rolodex to me with so much generosity; Juanita Villegas, Dania Becerra, and Monica Ordonez for helping to organize my ideas; and Julia Dangond for taking the time to listen to my dream at the beginning of this journey.

   I would also like to thank my family and friends: Gustavo Arango; Eva Hahn; Iran Issa Khan; Katia Gonzalez Ripoll; Graciela Robles; Jose Pascual; Milagros Maldonado; Gert and Ulla Elfering; Michael Gitter; Christopher Mason; Nicanor Cardenosa; Susan and Celia Bribragher; Mariangela Capuzzo; Jeff Kljajich; Sam Robin; Atilla Ata Uygun; Rhea Landig; Davi Abramson and David Zinsser; Patrick O'Shea; Lloyd Pollack; Nadine Johnson; Ken Harvey; Norman Wick Blood; Rob and

Terry Schechter; Juan C. Torres at Mellon Bank; Samuel Keller; Alberto Chehebar; Santiago Barbieri; Natalia Lanza; Antonio da Motta; Paul Meleschnig; Gingi Beltran; Dayssi Olarte de Kanavos; Walib and Susie Wahab; Adriana Arenas; La Gorda Puerta; Diego, Mercedes, and Mauricio from El Techo Restaurant; Andres Arias; Carlos Martorell; Fiona Ferrer and Jamie Polanco; Lolo Sudarsky; Sandra Merchan; Claudia Azuero; Juan Gallo and Gloria Saldarriaga; Tatiana Angel and Chiche Cayon; Andrea Alvarado at Stanford Trust; Celso Castro, Josefina Castro, and Gabriel Ossa; Catalina Casas; Ivonne Salcedo; Roberto Posada; Ingrid Hoffman; and the Dacosta Gomez family.

Locations, Stores, Fashion Designers, and Models: Patrick Vaysse, Benoit Delgrange, Carmen Otero, chef Simon Karl Buhler, and Sthepane Menou at Hotel Sofitel Santa Clara (www.HotelSantaClara.com); Maria Fernanda Santos and the staff at Hotel Majagua (www.hotelmajagua.com); Juan B. Sanint and Andrea Romero; Gustavo Pinto and Sergio Castano at Hotel Agua (www.hotelagua.com.co); Andrea Villegas at Casa del Mar (www.CasadelMar3662.com); Carlos Dunayer and Paola Mancini at Isla Rosa; Mario and Connie Pacheco; Hotel Boutique's El Marques and El Arzobispado; Carlos Cubillos and Pedro Ruiz; Patricia Nieto at Koralia (www.Koralia.com); Hacienda Quinta Santa Pedro Alejandrino; Isabelita Mejia at Hacienda San Jose; Claude Lamer, Fernando Echeverry, and Jenaro Mejia; Flora Nostra, Luz Maria Zuluaga, Maria Elena de Zapata, Amparo Jaramillo, Rosa Elena Angel, and Rodrigo Vega; Alberto Santamaria and Francisco Diaz; Camilo Holgin at Arquitectura Nativa (www.arquitecturanativa.com); Luz Miriam Toro, Belisario Betancourt, and Dalita Navarro; Moncha Mejia, Luis Alberto Martin, Jose Maria Rodrigez, and Ivon Valencia; Caridad and Gabriel; Mary Becerra Gomez; architect Simon Velez; Andres and Estella Jaramillo at Restaurant Andres Carne de Res (www.AndresCarnedeRes.com); Claudia Valenzuela and family; Dora de German Ribon; the Soto family at Hacienda Los Laureles; Arcanos Restaurant; Olga Pumarejo; Paola Morales; Ana Maria Fries; Cristina Meira at Cachivaches (www.Cachivaches.com); Carmenza de Arboleda at Dupuis Colombia; Aida Furmanski at Galena (www.Galenagift.com); Antiquario La Candelaria and Duna Muebles (www.Dunamuebles.com); decorator Alex Garcia. Fashion Designers: Mercedes Salazar (www.MercedesSalazar.com); Lina Cantillo (www.LinaCantillo.com); Jack Saad at Latino Royalty (www.LatinoRoyalty.com); Hernan Zajar. Models: La Agencia Models (www.Laagenciamodels.com) and FP Casting (www.fpcastingctg.com).